INFANT BAPTISM
IN THE FIRST FOUR
CENTURIES

THE LIBRARY OF HISTORY AND DOCTRINE

The aim of this international Library is to enable scholars to answer questions about the development of the Christian tradition which are important for an understanding of Christianity today

INFANT BAPTISM IN THE FIRST FOUR CENTURIES

JOACHIM JEREMIAS

Professor of Theology
in the University of Göttingen

Translated by
DAVID CAIRNS

Philadelphia
The Westminster Press

Translated from the German
Die Kindertaufe in den ersten vier Jahrhunderten
(published 1958 by Vandenhoeck & Ruprecht, Göttingen)
with new material by the author

Library of Congress Catalog Card No. 61-5625

PRINTED IN GREAT BRITAIN

CONTENTS

ILLUSTRATIONS

To the Theological Faculty
of Uppsala University
as a sign of respect and gratitude
for their conferring upon the author
the degree of Doctor of Theology

PREFACE

THE PRESENT book has developed out of a short pamphlet entitled *Hat die älteste Christenheit die Kindertaufe geübt?* (Did the primitive Church practise infant baptism?) (Göttingen, 1938; 2nd edition 1949). It does not attempt to do more than lay before the reader the historical material relating to the history of infant baptism in the first four centuries in as concrete and sober a manner as possible. This material has increased in an unexpected manner in the last decades. In this context I refer principally to the enrichment of our knowledge about proselyte baptism, the studies made of early Christian epitaphs, the ascription of the so-called *Egyptian Church Order* to Hippolytus, and the ascription to Asterius of some homilies on the Psalms which previously had wrongly been attributed to Chrysostom. Although much remains obscure, especially in the matter of its first beginnings, it may still be said that the early history of infant baptism is much more clearly defined today than in any previous age.

As compared with the German edition of this book, Chapter 2 has been worked over and rearranged. In particular, the comments on I Cor. 7.14c have been revised; I no longer venture to draw the conclusion that I Cor. 7.14c presupposes that the Christians of Corinth forebore to baptize the children of Christian parents.

I wish to express my warm thanks to the Rev. Professor David Cairns, D.D., of Christ's College, Aberdeen, for his excellent translation, to the Rev. Professor Henry Chadwick, D.D., of Oxford, for kindly placing at my disposal a list of the editions and translations used in Britain and the USA, and to Miss Jean Cunningham, Editorial Assistant, SCM Press, for the great care with which she prepared the typescript.

JOACHIM JEREMIAS

Göttingen,
January 1960

THE SOURCES

Texts which expressly mention infant baptism are marked with an asterisk.*

Year

54   1. I Cor. 1.16 see pp. 19, 21

75/80   2. Acts 2. 38 f.; 16.15, 33; 18.8; cf. 11.14 see pp. 19-23, 40 f.

112/13   3. PLINY THE YOUNGER, *Ep.* X 96 (to Trajan) 2, 9
            see pp. 63 f.
            Text and Translation: W. H. L. Hutchinson, Pliny,
            Letters, Melmouth's tr. (1746) revised, vol. II (Loeb
            59).

117/38   4. ARISTIDES OF ATHENS, *Apology* 15.11 see pp. 70 f.
            Syriac. Text: J. R. Harris and J. A. Robinson, *The*
            Apology of Aristides on behalf of the Christians (TS 1, 1),
            Cambridge, 1891. Translation: Harris and Robinson,
            pp. 35-51; ANCL, Additional Volume, ed. A.
            Menzies, Edinburgh, 1897.
            Greek papyrus fragments. Text: B. P. Grenfell
            and A. S. Hunt, *The Oxyrhynchus Papyri* XV (Egypt
            Exploration Society [Graeco-Roman Memoirs 18]),
            London, 1922, pp. 1-6. Plate I (No. 1778; *Apol.* 5.4;
            6.1, 2). H. J. M. Milne, 'A New Fragment of the
            Apology of Aristides', *JTS* 25, 1923/24, pp. 73-77
            (Br. Mus. Gr. Pap. 2486; *Apol.* 15.6-16.1).

before 150   5. Acts 2.39 D see p. 72

150/55   6. JUSTIN MARTYR, *Apology* I 15.6 see p. 72
            Text: *MPG* 6, 349; *The Apologies of Justin Martyr*,
            ed. A. W. F. Blunt, Cambridge, 1911. Translation:
            ANCL 2, 1867; E. R. Hardy, 'The First Apology
            of Justin, the Martyr', in *Early Christian Fathers*
            (Library of Christian Classics I), London, 1953,
            pp. 242-289.

c. 165   *Acts of Justin and his Companions* 4.5–7   see p. 64
Text: R. Knopf and G. Krüger, *Ausgewählte Märtyrer-
akten* (Sammlung ausgewählter kirchen- und dogmengeschichtlicher Quellenschriften, N.F.3)³, Tübingen, 1929, p. 16.27–32. Translation: E. C. E. Owen,
Some Authentic Acts of the Early Martyrs, Oxford,
1927, p. 50

167/68   7. *Martyrdom of Polycarp* 9.3   see pp. 59–63
Text: *MPG* 5, 1036. Text and Translation: J. B.
Lightfoot and J. R. Harmer, *The Apostolic Fathers*,
London and New York, 1891; K. Lake, *The Apostolic
Fathers*, vol. II (Loeb 25). Translation only: J.
Goodspeed, *The Apostolic Fathers*: An American
Translation, New York, 1950; M. H. Shepherd,
'Martyrdom of Polycarp as told in the Letter of the
Church of Smyrna to the Church of Philomelium',
in *Early Christian Fathers*, pp. 141–158.

161/80   8. *Acts of Carpus, Papylus and Agathonica* 34   see p. 64
Text: R. Knopf and G. Krüger, *op. cit.*, p. 12.26 f.
Translation: E. C. E. Owen, *op. cit.*, p. 45

after 180   9. IRENAEUS OF LYONS, *Adversus Haereses* II 22.4 *MPG*
= II 33.2 Harvey   see pp. 73 f.
Text: *MPG* 7, 784; W. W. Harvey, *Sancti Irenaei
episcopi Lugdunensis libri quinque adversus haereses* I,
Cambridge, 1857, p. 330.9–21. Translation (II
22.4): ANCL 5, 1868; M. Hitchcock, *Irenaeus,
Treatise against the Heresies*, 2 vols., London,
1916.

190/91   10. POLYCRATES OF EPHESUS, *Ep. to Victor of Rome*, in:
Eusebius, *Historia Ecclesiastica* V 24.6 f.   see p. 63
Text: *MPG* 20, 496 f. Text and Translation: K. Lake
and J. E. L. Oulton, *Eusebius, Ecclesiastical History*,
vol. I (Loeb 153). Translation only: H. J. Lawlor and
J. E. L. Oulton, *Eusebius Pamphili, The Ecclesiastical
History and the Martyrs of Palestine*, 2 vols., London,
1952/53; NPNF (2nd ser.) 1, 1904.

195   11. CLEMENT OF ALEXANDRIA, *Paedagogus* III 59.2   see p. 64
Text: *MPG* 8, 633; O. Stählin, *Clemens Alexandrinus
I: Protrepticus und Paedagogus (GCS* 12)², Leipzig,
1936, p. 270.10 f. Translation: ANCL 4, 1867.

c. 200 or soon after	12.	*Inscription of Eutychianus* (Rome) see p. 76

Text: *ILCV* I 1611 C. F. J. Dölger, *IXΘYC* I², pp. 192–197. See illustration p. 76.

200/06   13. *TERTULLIAN, *De Baptismo* 18.3–6 see pp. 81–84

Text: *MPL* 1, 1221 f.; R. F. Refoulé and M. Drouzy, *Tertullien. Traité du Baptême* (SC 35), Paris, 1952, pp. 92.12–93.12; J. G. Ph. Borleffs, *Q.S.Fl. Tertulliani De baptismo* (Corpus Christianorum: Series Latina 1.8), Turnhout, 1954, p. 293. Translation: ANCL 11, 1859.

210/13   TERTULLIAN, *De Anima* 39.4 see pp. 84 f.

Text: *MPL* 2, 718; J. H. Waszink, *Quinti Septimi Florentis Tertulliani De Anima*, Amsterdam, 1947, p. 56.6–14; idem, *Q.S.Fl. Tertulliani De anima* (Corpus Christianorum: Series Latina 2.17), Turnhout, 1954, pp. 842 f. Translation: ANCL 15, 1870.

c. 215   14. *HIPPOLYTUS OF ROME, *Apostolic Tradition* 21.3 f. see pp. 73–75, 91 f.

The *Apostolic Tradition* of Hippolytus is not preserved as a single work in the original Greek text or in translation, but was the source of many early books of church order which allow us to recover the original text. The most important of these are: an old Latin book of order (probably from the end of the fourth century), the *Egyptian Church Order* (perhaps *c.* AD 500, extant in Coptic, Arabic and Ethiopic translations), the *Testamentum Domini* extant in a Syriac translation (fifth century), the *Canons of Hippolytus* in an Arabic translation, and the eighth book of the *Apostolic Constitutions* (cf. No. 25). English translations of the conjectural original text with introduction and notes, based on all the available material, were published by B. S. Easton, Cambridge, 1934, and by G. Dix, London, 1937.

The rule for infant baptism (*Ap. Trad.* 21.3 f.) is preserved in:

Coptic: *Egyptian Church Order*, Can. 46. Text: W. Till and J. Leipoldt, *Der koptische Text der Kirchenordnung Hippolyts* (TU 58), Berlin, 1954. Translation: G. Horner, *The Statutes of Apostles or*

Canones Ecclesiastici, London, 1904, p. 316.23–27.
Arabic: *Egyptian Church Order*, Can. 34. Text:
Horner, p. 100.15–17. Translation: Horner, pp. 253.
10–13; 423. *Can. Hipp.* 19.7. Text: D. B. von Hane-
berg, *Canones S. Hippolyti arabice e codicibus Romanis*,
Munich, 1870, p. 39.14–16. German Translation:
W. Riedel, *Die Kirchenrechtsquellen des Patriarchats
Alexandrien*, Leipzig, 1900, p. 211.9–13.
Ethiopic: *Egyptian Church Order*, Can. 35. Text:
Horner, p. 21.12–15. Translation: Horner, pp.
152.24–27; 380.
Syriac: *Test. Dom.* II 8. Text: I. E. II Rahmani,
Testamentum Domini nostri Jesu Christi, Mainz, 1899,
p. 126.9–16. German tr.: Rahmani, p. 127. 10–18.

after 233   15. *ORIGEN, *In Lucam Homilia* 14 on 2.22 a   see p. 65
Text: *MPG* 13, 1835; M. Rauer, *Origenes Werke* IX.
*Die Homilien zu Lukas in der Übersetzung des Hierony-
mus und die griechischen Reste der Homilien und des
Lukaskommentars* (*GCS* 35), Leipzig, 1930,p.98.10–23.

after 244   *ORIGEN, *Commentarius in Epistulam ad Romanos*
V 9 on 6.5–7   see p. 65
Text: *MPG* 14, 1047; C. H. E. Lommatzsch, *Origenis
in Epistulam ad Romanos Commentariorum* Pars I
(*Origenis Opera omnia* 6), Berlin, 1836, p. 397.18 f.

after 244   *ORIGEN, *In Leviticum Homilia* 8.3 on 12.2 see p. 65
Text: *MPG* 12, 496; W. A. Baehrens, *Origenes Werke*
VI. *Homilien zum Hexateuch in Rufins Übersetzung* I:
Die Homilien zu Genesis, Exodus und Leviticus (*GCS*
29), Leipzig, 1920, p. 398.10–13.

after 244   ORIGEN, *Commentary on Matthew* XV 36 on
20.1–16   see pp. 65 f. n. 5
Text: *MPG* 13, 1360; E. Klostermann, *Origenes
Werke* X. *Origenes Matthäuserklärung* I. *Die griechisch
erhaltenen Tomoi* (*GCS* 40), Leipzig, 1935, p. 457a.
7–9; 458 a.9.

249/51   *ORIGEN, *In Jesum Nave homilia* 9.4 on 8.32 see. pp 65 f.
Text: *MPG* 12, 874; W. A. Baehrens, *Origenes Werke*
VII. *Homilien zum Hexateuch in Rufins Übersetzung*
II: *Die Homilien zu Numeri, Josua und Judices* (*GCS*
30), Leipzig, 1921, p. 350.2–8.

251 16. *CYPRIAN OF CARTHAGE, *De lapsis* 9   see p. 85
Text: *MPL* 4, 473; G. Hartel, *S. Thasci Caecili Cypriani Opera omnia* [I] (*CSEL* 3.1), Vienna, 1868, p. 243.7–18. Translation: ANCL 8, 1868.

251 or 253   *CYPRIAN, *Ep.* 64 (to Fidus). 2–6   see p. 85
Text: *MPL* 3, 1015–19; G. Hartel, *S. Thasci Caecili Cypriani Opera omnia* [II] (*CSEL* 3.2), Vienna, 1871, pp. 718–721. Translation: ANCL 8, 1868.

3rd century 17. *Epitaphs* from 3rd century   see pp. 74–80, 85

3rd century 18. *Mummy of Child* Br. Mus. 54051 (Egypt)   see pp. 66–68
Previously unpublished. See illustration facing p. 64.

306/12 19. SYNOD OF ELVIRA (Southern Spain), *Canons*
I, 22   see p. 92
Text: Hardouin I 249, 252; F. Lauchert, *Die Kanones der wichtigsten altkirchlichen Concilien nebst den Apostolischen Kanones* (Sammlung ausgewählter kirchen- und dogmengeschichtlicher Quellenschriften 12), Freiburg and Tübingen, 1896, pp. 13, 17.

†after 341 20. *ASTERIUS THE SOPHIST, *Homilies on the Psalms*
12.3–7; 21.10; 27.2 f.   see p. 93
Text: *MPG* 40, 445, 448; M. Richard, *Asterii Sophistae commentariorum in Psalmos quae supersunt* (Symbolae Osloenses fasc. supplet. XVI), Oslo, 1956, pp. 82–84, 163, 215.

c. 365 21. *OPTATUS OF MILEVIS, *Contra Parmenianum Donatistam libri VII*, V 10   see p. 94
Text: *MPL* 11, 1063; C. Ziwsa, *S. Optati Milevitani Libri VII* (*CSEL* 26), Vienna, Prague and Leipzig, 1893, p. 140.10–19. Translation: O. R. Vassall-Phillips, *The Work of St Optatus, Bishop of Milevis, Against the Donatists*, London, 1917.

362/72 22. *ZENO OF VERONA, *Tractatus* I 13   see p. 94, nn. 5 and 9
Text: *MPL* 11, 354.

371/72 23. *BASIL THE GREAT, according to Theodoret of Cyrus, *Historia ecclesiastica* (449/50) IV 19.8–10
see pp. 91 f. n. 7.
Text: *MPG* 82, 1162; L. Parmentier and F. Scheidweiler, *Theodoret Kirchengeschichte*[2] (*GCS* 44 [19]), Berlin, 1954, p. 244.7–19. Translation: NPNF (2nd ser.) 3, 1892.

before 380 24. *Pseudo-Clementine Homilies* 13.4.4 par. *Re-cognitions* 7.29; *Hom.* 15.1.2 par. *Recognitions* 10.1–4   see pp. 68 f.
Text: *Homilies: MPG* 2, 332, 356; B. Rehm, *Die Pseudoklementinen* I: *Homilien* (*GCS* 42), Berlin, 1953, pp. 194.16–18; 212.5 f. *Recognitions: MPG* 1, 1367, 1419–1422. Translation: *Homilies*: ANCL 17, 1870. *Recognitions*: ANCL 3, 1867.

c. 380   25. **Apostolic Constitutions* VI 15.7   see pp. 69, 92 n. 5
Text: *MPG* 1, 949; F. X. Funk, *Didascalia et Con-stitutiones Apostolorum* I, Paderborn, 1906, p. 339.8. Translation: ANCL 17, 1870.

7.1.381   26. **GREGORY OF NAZIANZUS, Oratio,* 40.17, 23, 28
see pp. 89, 95 f.
Text: *MPG* 36, 380 f., 389, 400. Translation: NPNF (2nd. ser.) VII, 1894.

10.2.385 27. **POPE SIRICIUS, Ep.* 1 (to Himerius of Tarra-gona) 2.3   see pp. 74 n. 1, 94 nn. 5 f.
Text: *MPL* 13, 1134 f.

387   28. **AMBROSE OF MILAN, De Abraham* II 11.79–81, 84
see pp. 94 f.
Text: *MPL* 14, 494 f., 497; C. Schenkl, *Sancti Ambrosii Opera* I (*CSEL* 32.1 II), Vienna, Prague and Leipzig, 1897, pp. 631–633; 635.

385/89   **AMBROSE OF MILAN, Expositio Evangelii secundum Lucam* I 36–38 on 1.17   see p. 94 n. 5
Text: *MPL* 15, 1548 f.; C. Schenkl, *Sancti Ambrosii Opera* IV (*CSEL* 32.4), Vienna, Prague and Leipzig, 1902, pp. 32–34.

388   29. **JOHN CHRYSOSTOM, In Genesim homilia* 40.4
see p. 94 n. 7
Text: *MPG* 53, 373.
*JOHN CHRYSOSTOM, Homilia ad neophytos, in: Augustine, *Contra Iulianum Pelagianum* I 6.21 f.   see p. 95
Text: *MPL* 44, 654–56.

381/92   30. **DIDYMUS THE BLIND (Alexandria), De trini-tate* II 14   see p. 95
Text: *MPG* 39, 708.

397   31. *THIRD SYNOD OF CARTHAGE, *Canon* 48   see p. 94
             Text: Hardouin I 968; F. Lauchert, *op. cit.*, pp. 173 f.

4th century 32. *Epitaphs* of the 4th century   see pp. 89–91, 92 f.

c. 400   33. *JEROME, *Ep.* 107 (to Laeta). 6   see p. 95
             Text: *MPL* 22, 873; I. Hilberg, *Sancti Eusebii Hier-*
             onymi Epistulae II (*CSEL* 55), Vienna and Leipzig,
             1912, pp. 297 f. Translation: NPNF (2nd ser.) 6,
             1893.

415   *JEROME, *Dialogus adversus Pelagianos* III 17–19
             Text: *MPL* 23, 586–590. Translation: NPNF (2nd
             ser.) 6, 1893.

Sept. 401 34. *SIXTH SYNOD OF CARTHAGE, *Canon* 7   see p. 94 n. 5
             Text: Hardouin I 987 (Canon 6).

402   35. *SNYOD OF ROME, *Canon* 5   see p. 94 n. 5
             Text: Hardouin I 1035.

before 406 36. *CRESCONIUS DONATISTA, in: Augustine, *Contra*
             Cresconium Grammaticum et Donatistam I 31.36
                                 see pp. 48, 93 f.
             Text: *MPL* 43, 465; M. Petschenig, *Sancti Aureli*
             Augustini Scripta contra Donatistas II (*CSEL* 52),
             Vienna and Leipzig, 1909, pp. 355.28–356.2

c. 415   37. *INNOCENT I, *Ep.* 3 (to the Synod of Toledo)
             6.10   see p. 94 n. 5
             Text: *MPL* 20, 492; Hardouin I 1020 f. (No. 23.5).

416   *INNOCENT I, *Ep.* 25 (to Decentius of Eugubium)
             3.6   see p. 94 n. 5
             Text: *MPL* 20, 554 f.; Hardouin I 997 (No. 1.3).

412   *INNOCENT I, *Ep.* 30 (to the second Synod of
             Milevis). 5   see p. 94 n. 5
             Text: *MPL* 20, 592; Hardouin I 1029 (No. 25).

418   38. *SIXTEENTH SYNOD OF CARTHAGE, *Canons* 2, 3 see p. 96
             Text: Hardouin I 927 f., 1217 f.

after 420 39. *MARK THE DEACON, *Vita Porphyrii episcopi*
             Gazensis 31, 47   see p. 95 n. 2
             Text: Societatis Philologae Bonnensis Sodales, *Marci*
             Diaconi Vita Porphyrii episcopi Gazensis (Bibliotheca
             Scriptorum Graecorum et Romanorum Teubneriana
             [63⁹], Leipzig, 1895, pp. 29.6–9; 41.3–42.5. Text and
             French Translation: H. Grégoire and M. A. Kugener,

B

Marc Le Diacre, Vie de Porphyre, évêque de Gaza.
Text établi, traduit et commenté Coll. Budé, Paris,
1930. Translation: G. F. Hill, *Life of Porphyry, Mark
the Deacon*, Oxford, 1913.

†430   40. *AUGUSTINE in many writings   cf. pp. 94–7

I

The Baptism of Children of Parents joining the Church in the Earliest Period

THE NEW TESTAMENT was written in a missionary situation. It is therefore not surprising that we should have to note at the outset that all New Testament statements about baptism without exception relate to missionary baptism—i.e. baptism administered when Jews and Gentiles were received into the fellowship.

If we realize this fact, we shall understand why, in the New Testament statements about baptism, the conversion of adults and their baptism stands right in the middle of the picture. For it is they who are joining the Church, while the children, who are, as it were, hidden in the bosom of the family, cannot claim the same degree of attention. This makes the task which engages us more difficult. Yet luckily we are not entirely without material which enables us to infer an answer to the question 'Were the children of converts baptized along with their parents?'

I. THE OIKOS FORMULA

Here first we must mention the passages which speak of the conversion and baptism of a 'household': I Cor. 1.16: 'I did baptize also the household of Stephanas'; Acts 16.15: the half-proselyte Lydia 'was baptized with her household'; 16.33: the keeper of the prison in Philippi 'was baptized . . . with all his family'; 18.8: 'Crispus, the ruler of the synagogue, believed in the Lord, together with all his household; and many of the Corinthians hearing Paul believed and were baptized'; cf. also 11.14: 'You will be saved, you and all your household.' In the case of Crispus the leader of the synagogue and perhaps also in that of Stephanas[1] we have

[1] A. Schlatter, *Paulus der Bote Jesu*, Stuttgart, 1934, p. 12, is too confident in his conclusion: 'Stephanas was a Jew.'

to do with a Jewish 'household', in the other cases with the 'households' of half-proselytes and Gentiles. What in such cases was commonly understood by οἶκος is shown by Ign. *Smyrn.* 13.1: 'Greetings to the families of my brothers, along with their wives and children'; i.e. father and mother of the household and children of all ages.[1] In addition relatives living in the house and the servants were counted as belonging to the household.[2]

If we now ask whether in the passages cited, which speak of a 'house' joining the Church and being baptized, the baptism of children and infants is also thought of, a provisional answer to our question is indicated when we observe that οἶκος can be replaced by ὅλος ὁ οἶκος, πᾶς ὁ οἶκος (the whole house), οἱ αὐτοῦ ἅπαντες (all of his). The addition of ὅλος, πᾶς, ἅπαντες (the whole, all) makes it quite clear that no single member of the household was excluded from baptism; and in view of the general sociological picture we have received of the oldest communities of the missionary church, it is extremely unlikely that the households of Cornelius, of the keeper of the prison in Philippi, of Lydia, of Crispus the leader of the synagogue and of Stephanas ever included a considerable group of slaves, to whom the words ὅλος, πᾶς, ἅπαντες could refer. Accordingly the natural conclusion is that we should take these additional terms to refer to all the children of the house.

Old Testament terminology confirms this conclusion. To Stauffer belongs the credit of investigating, in the article just mentioned, the Old Testament material in order to throw light on the New Testament passages that speak of the baptism of 'a whole household'—a task which, incredible to relate, no one had attempted before.

In the Old Testament we find with many variations the formula 'He and his (whole) house', and the investigation of this rich material led Stauffer to the conclusion that from early times there was a constant biblical 'oikos formula' which 'not only referred to the children in addition to the adults but had quite *special* reference to the children, and not least to any *small children* who might be present'.[3] When—to begin with secular instances—Ahimelech was threatened by Saul that he and 'all his father's

---

[1] In the much discussed passage, Ign., *Polyc.* 8. 2, ἀσπάζομαι . . . τὴν τοῦ Ἐπιτρόπου σὺν ὅλῳ τῷ οἴκῳ αὐτῆς καὶ τῶν τέκνων, 'I greet the (widow) of Epitropos with all the members of her and her children's household,' the τέκνα are grown-up children who already have their own households (E. Stauffer, 'Zur Kindertaufe in der Urkirche', *Deutsches Pfarrerblatt* 49, 1949, p. 152 n. 2; A. Oepke, Review of J. Schneider's *Die Taufe im Neuen Testament*, Stuttgart, 1952, *TLZ* 79, col. 103). Thus the word οἶκος does not refer to the household without the children, but several households are greeted, the household of the widow and those of her married children.

[2] Day-labourers, on the other hand, were not reckoned in Palestine to belong to the bᵉne bhayith (Ma'as. 3.1) since they did not live in the house.

[3] *Op. cit.*, p. 153; Stauffer's italics.

house' must die (I Sam. 22.16), and when in execution of this threat the whole priestly town of Nob was extirpated, except one fugitive, the horror of this act of vengeance is revealed by the fact that not even the little children and infants were spared (v. 19: children and sucklings). Or when Pharaoh gave Joseph's brothers permission to bring their father and their 'households' to Egypt (Gen. 45.18), the scope of his solicitude is illustrated by his supplying carriages for the women and for those who 'could not' (no longer or not yet) 'walk'—that is, for the old people and children[1] (v. 19) so that none need stay behind. Accepting the invitation, Jacob travelled with his whole clan to Egypt, and it is made clear to the reader that they all really accompanied him by the statement that grandsons and granddaughters were taken with him (46.7). Again, in the use of the *oikos* formula in a ritual sense to elucidate the whole content of the concept of 'household', the emphasis falls on the inclusion of even the very youngest members. Every year Elkanah travels 'with his whole household' to Shiloh to make sacrifice (I Sam. 1.21); it is mentioned, as an exception, that Hannah with her as yet unweaned baby stays behind (v. 22). We can see especially clearly from the instructions for circumcision how the *oikos* formula lays emphasis on the inclusion of the smallest children: 'every male among the men of Abraham's house' was circumcised (Gen. 17.23), that is, all the male members of the household down to the babies 'eight days old' (v. 12).

When after these observations we turn to the New Testament, we must keep in mind that the New Testament *oikos* formula is very early. It occurs as early as AD 54 in Paul (I Cor. 1.16), and is to be found independently of Paul in Luke, and is therefore to be regarded as a pre-Pauline formula. Thus it comes from a time in which the majority of the members of the churches came from the synagogue and from the circle of the 'God-fearers' loosely attached thereto. If we grasp this, we shall have to agree with Stauffer's conclusion, that the New Testament *oikos* formula was adopted from the Old Testament cultic language (and in particular, we may say, from the terminology of circumcision) and introduced into the formal language employed in the primitive Christian rite of baptism; it has the same form and the same meaning as the old biblical ritual formula, i.e. it includes small children as well as others.[2] This does not mean to say that in every particular case in which the baptism of 'a whole household' is mentioned, small children were actually present. But it does mean that Paul and Luke could under no circumstances have applied the *oikos*

---

[1] *hattaph.*
[2] Stauffer, *op. cit.*, p. 153.

formula, if they had wished to say that only adults had been baptized.[1] Quite a different set of considerations leads us to the same result. New inquiries have shown us what significance 'corporate personality'[2] has had for the thinking of the Bible, and how great a part *family solidarity* played in the ancient world.[3] If we wish to understand biblical texts rightly, we must radically free ourselves from modern individualistic thinking, and in particular keep before our eyes the fact that the family represented by the father of the household was in old times much more strongly experienced as a unity than today. People felt the solidarity, the mutual responsibility and the unity of the group. All important questions were decided by the father of the household and his decision was binding on all. In particular in its relation to God the household was a unity. Correspondingly it was normal for the ancient mind to regard the faith of the father of the household as decisive, if a household broke away from the old religious community and embraced a new religion. Doubtless from an early time there were mixed marriages,[4] because only one of the partners had been laid hold of by the Gospel, but in such cases, as in Jewish missions, it was commonly the woman who alone changed her religion.[5] If the father of the household became a Christian, the family followed him, not indeed always,[6] but usually. Acts 16.30–34 provides an instructive example of the part which the father of the household played when a family changed its religion. The keeper of the prison asks Paul and Silas, 'Sirs, what must I (sing.) do that I (sing.) may be saved?' (v. 30). And they said, 'Believe (sing.) on the Lord Jesus and thou shalt be saved, *and thy house*' (v. 31). 'And they spake unto him the word of the Lord, and to all that were in his house (v. 32). And he took them the same hour of the night, and washed their stripes; and was baptized, he and all his, straightway (v. 33). And when he had brought them into his house, he set meat before them, and rejoiced (sing.) that he (sing.) *had come to*

---

[1] Cf. Théo Preiss, 'Die Kindertaufe und das Neue Testament', *TLZ* 73, 1948, col. 657.

[2] Cf. the reports on research given by A. Bentzen, *King and Messiah*, ET London, 1955, and by North, *The Suffering Servant in Deutero-Isaiah*, London, 1948. See also E. Percy, *Der Leib Christi (Σῶμα Χριστοῦ) in den paulinischen Homologumena und Antilegomena* (Lunds Universitets Årsskrift, N.F. Avd. 1, 38: 1), Lund and Leipzig, 1942.

[3] E. Ménégoz, 'Le baptême des enfants d'après les principes de la théologie paulinienne', *Revue Chrétienne* 31, 1884, p. 236; H. Grossmann, *Ein Ja zur Kindertaufe* (Kirchliche Zeitfragen 13), Zürich, 1944, pp. 19–22; O. Cullmann, *Baptism in the New Testament*, ET (SBT 1), London, 1950, p. 45.

[4] I Cor. 7.12–16; I Peter 3.1 and perhaps a similar case in Titus 2.5; cf. J. Jeremias, 'Die missionarische Aufgabe in der Mischehe (I Cor. 7.16)', in *Neutestamentliche Studien für Rudolf Bultmann* (BZNW 21), Berlin, 1954, pp. 255–60.

[5] II Tim. 1.5; Titus 2.5; I Peter 3.1; the Apronianus inscription is also instructive (see pp. 41 f.).

[6] I Cor. 7.12.

faith in God' (v. 34). The conversion of the father of the household implies the salvation of the household and is cause for the joy of the members of the household. The situation in Acts 16.14 f. is quite similar: Lydia who, we may assume, as a widow is the head of her household, is converted and thereupon 'she and her house' are baptized. Certainly that is a condensed report, which omits the statement that the good news was also proclaimed to the members of Lydia's household and that they believed in it; but even granted this, it is characteristic that Luke could report the matter thus. For by so doing he gives expression to the fact that *'the solidarity of the family in baptism* and not the individual decision of the single member' was the decisive consideration.[1] But when we consider family solidarity resting upon the authoritative influence of the head of the family it is scarcely conceivable that the baptism of a 'household' did not include all its members.[2] How much the corporate change of religion by a family was taken for granted can be seen from the regulation which was observed in certain Jewish-Christian circles, that the unbaptized members of the family must be excluded from the table-fellowship of the family;[3] this regulation shows that the possibility that the children might not be baptized along with their parents was not contemplated at all. The way in which the solidarity of the family was taken for granted explains further why no reason was found for emphasizing or justifying especially the baptism of children.[4]

In conclusion, reference must be made to the fact that baptism in the primitive church was an *eschatological sacrament*. It meant that the person baptized was snatched out of a world delivered over to the immediately impending judgment of God (Acts 2.38; Col. 1.13) and incorporated into the company of those redeemed by Christ's saving work, an eschatological sealing in the last hour before the catastrophe. A division within the families joining the church by reason of a difference of age is, in these circumstances, highly improbable.

Theologically, the establishment of the fact that children were baptized as members of a family joining the church, is of fundamental significance. The children were not regarded by the primitive church as isolated units;

---

[1] Cullmann, *op. cit.*, p. 45; his italics.
[2] Preiss, *op. cit.*, col. 652 f., concludes rightly that infant baptism in the Church of the first centuries is closely related to the problem of the Christian family. Oepke, 'Die Kindertaufe—eine Wunde unserer Kirche?', *Evangelisch-Lutherische Kirchenzeitung* 1, 1947, p. 32, and Cullmann, *op. cit.*, p. 45, both referred at the same time in this connection to the fact that in I Cor. 10.1 f. a baptismal grace is presupposed which is shared by a whole community as such, including all its children.
[3] See below, pp. 68 f.
[4] It should be remembered how seldom in the OT the circumcision of male infants is expressly mentioned.

the household was regarded as a unity in the sight of God. The faith of the father who represents the household and the faith of the mother embraces also the children.

2. PRIMITIVE CHRISTIAN BAPTISM AND PROSELYTE BAPTISM

To none of the innumerable lustration rites of adjoining or more distant lands[1] is primitive Christian baptism so akin as it is to proselyte baptism. It is therefore of importance for the problem which concerns us to find out what happened to children and babies in proselyte baptism. It is however uncertain at what date proselyte baptism was introduced. Although the many points of similarity between primitive Christian baptism and proselyte baptism, on which we shall have to touch, constitute in themselves an indirect proof of the existence of proselyte baptism in New Testament times, because an influence of the Christian rite on the Jewish one must be excluded as impossible, yet a prefatory note is necessary on the date when proselyte baptism was introduced.

A. The date of the introduction of proselyte baptism

The Old Testament knows nothing of a custom of subjecting a converted heathen to the rite of baptism. Even Philo and Josephus make no mention of proselyte baptism. As far as was known hitherto, it first appears in rabbinic texts, and there in a discussion of the schools of Shammai and Hillel to which we must refer again;[2] the texts belong to the time before the destruction of Jerusalem (AD 70). Apart from rabbinic sources proselyte baptism is mentioned in *Orac. Sib.* IV. 162–70 (about AD 80)[3] and again by Epictetus (about AD 94).[4] The story of a distinguished lady of the name of Valeria who was baptized along with her female slaves[5] takes us back to the time before the Bar-Cochba Rebellion (i.e. before AD 135).[6] If we survey this list of the oldest references hitherto known, we shall understand how the silence of Philo and

---

[1] A survey is to be found in E. Lohmeyer's *Das Urchristentum*, 1, *Johannes der Täufer*, Göttingen, 1932, p. 145.

[2] Pes. 8.8 par. 'Éduy. 5.2; b. Pes. 92a. Compare further Tos. Pes. 7.13 (ed. Zuckermandel, 1908, p. 167) and parallels. See below, pp. 28 f.

[3] See below, p. 34 with note 2.

[4] *Dissertations* II 9.19–21. In order to understand the passage in Epictetus we must note that τὸ πάθος (ὅταν δ'ἀναλάβῃ τὸ πάθος τὸ τοῦ βεβαμμένου) really means circumcision; cf. G. Polster, 'Der kleine Talmudtraktat über die Proselyten', *Angelos* 2, 1926, p. 21 n. 1; J. Thomas, *Le mouvement baptiste en Palestine et Syrie (150 av. J.-Chr.-300 ap. J.-Chr.*), Gembloux, 1935, p. 361 n. 3.

[5] Mekh. Ex. 12.48.

[6] A. Schlatter, *Geschichte Israels von Alexander dem Grossen bis Hadrian*[3], Stuttgart, 1925, p. 439.

Josephus have occasionally given rise to doubts whether proselyte baptism goes back so far as the days of the early Church.

And yet there are the most varied grounds for holding to this early date. We place the most decisive consideration first. The Torah was binding on Israel alone. The Old Testament regulations about Levitical purity and impurity were consequently binding on Israelites exclusively. According to the older view, demonstrably still dominant as late as the third century AD, a Gentile who was not under the law could not be legally impure.[1] Only his idols, already in the days of the prophets, were reckoned impure.[2] If Pharisaic circles—as we hear from Daniel,[3] Tobit[4] and Judith[5]—avoided the food and drink of Gentiles from the second century BC onwards, it was not because they held the Gentiles to be Levitically impure, but because this food and drink might have come in touch with the heathen cultus and have been defiled by that contact (e.g. wine through libation, meat through sacrifice). All this is in agreement with the fact that in the second century BC circumcision was sufficient when a Gentile was converted to Judaism and nothing is said about baptism.[6] It is not until the end of the first century BC that people begin to reckon a Gentile personally impure. Obviously the intention is in this manner to prohibit mixed marriages of Jews with Gentiles,[7] and it is indeed the Hillelites who, in conflict with their more conservative opponents, the Shammaites, ascribe to a Gentile woman the permanent impurity of a menstruous person.[8] We are here in the fortunate position of being able to give a date. A report, very often repeated, tells how the High Priest Simeon, the son of Kamithos, could not perform his priestly duty on the Day of Atonement because on the previous evening as darkness fell (i.e. when it was too late to take a bath before sunset), he had been struck by the spittle of an Arab and thereby had been made unclean.[9] Simeon, the son of Kamithos, was High Priest in the year 17–18 AD. By that time accordingly the view of the Hillelites had won the day, for the

---

[1] b. Pes. 92a (R. Johanan, died 279); j. Pes. 8.36b. 31.

[2] Isa. 30.22; Jer. 2.7, 23; 3.2, 9; 7.30; Ezek. 36.18. Also later Jub. 22. 16 ff.; 'Aboda Zara 3.6; Shab. 9.1.

[3] Dan. 1.8, 12.

[4] Tob. 1.10 f.

[5] Judith 12.2.

[6] Judith 14.10: Achior.

[7] Cf. Test. Levi 14.6 (see below, pp. 26–28).

[8] 'Eduy. 5.1; Nid. 4.3.

[9] Tos. Yoma 4.20 (189); b. Yoma 47a; j. Yoma 1.38d. 6; i. Meg. 1.72a. 49; j. Hor. 3.47d. 11; Lev. r. 20.7 on 16.1 f; Num. r. 2.22 on 3.4; Tanḥ. 'aḥare moth (ed. Vienna, 1863, 164b. 32). The variant 'spittle of a Sadducee' (b. Nid. 33b Bar.; Tos. Nid. 5.3 [645]) is an anti-Sadducean correction, see J. Jeremias, *Jerusalem zur Zeit Jesu* II B 1, Leipzig, 1929, = ²Göttingen, 1958, p. 10 n. 3.

Arab is impure[1] because he is constantly made so by his wife, who is in a permanent condition of Nidda.[2] The further complicated history of the regulations concerning the impurity of the Gentiles, which is also important for the understanding of the Book of Acts, does not concern us here. Only we may remark that in many places in the New Testament the impurity of the Gentiles is presupposed.[3] What we have said shows with certainty that proselyte baptism reaches back to pre-Christian times; for in that moment in which it was acknowledged that the Gentiles were impure, the necessity of a bath of purification on conversion was admitted.

Starting from this firm chronological fact we are enabled to date a hitherto overlooked passage which, without mentioning the term, speaks of proselyte baptism and may represent the oldest evidence for its practice which we possess. The passage is Test. Levi 14.6:

> 'With harlots and adulteresses shall ye be joined, and the daughters of the Gentiles shall ye take to wife,
> Purifying them with unlawful purifications (καθαρίζοντες αὐτὰς καθαρισμῷ παρανόμῳ);
> And your union shall be like unto Sodom and Gomorrah.'

Two factors bearing on the dating of the Testament of the Twelve Patriarchs have recently come to the fore. First, M. de Jonge has disputed the usual view that the work is a Jewish writing of the beginning of the second century BC,[4] which then was probably interpolated by a Jewish hand[5] and certainly later by a Christian hand. De Jonge for his part takes up again the thesis which almost held a monopoly in the nineteenth century, that we have here to do with a Christian writing which uses Jewish sources, and he dates it to about 200 AD.[6] As far as our passage, Test. Levi 14.6, is concerned, this dispute need not detain us, for the Jewish character of this verse is evident from the veto on mixed marriages with Gentile women and is uncontested.[7] Secondly, the discoveries

---

[1] A. Büchler, 'The Levitical Impurity of the Gentile in Palestine before the year 70', *JQR* 17, 1926/27, pp. 1–81; here p. 8.

[2] A menstruous woman.

[3] Matt. 8.7 (to be read as a question); John 18.28; Acts 10.28; 11.12; I Cor. 7.14; cf. Gal. 2.12.

[4] So, recently, E. Bickerman, 'The date of the Testaments of the Twelve Patriarchs', *JBL* 69, 1950, pp. 245–60: 200–175 BC.

[5] As an example relevant to our passage we may cite W. Bousset, 'Die Testamente der zwölf Patriarchen II', *ZNW* 1, 1900, pp. 187–93, and R. H. Charles, *The Testaments of the Twelve Patriarchs*, London, 1908, pp. lvii, 54 f. They assign Test. Levi 14–16 to the later Maccabaean period, on account of the sharp threatening prophecies against Levi (Charles: 70–50 BC.).

[6] M. de Jonge, *The Testaments of the Twelve Patriarchs* (Van Gorcum's Theologische Bibliotheek 25), Assen, 1953.

[7] M. de Jonge, *op. cit.*, p. 127.

at Qumran have placed our general outlook on the Testaments of the Twelve Patriarchs on a new basis. Right at the beginning of the century Aramaic, Greek and Syriac fragments of an older form of the Testament of Levi[1] had been discovered. And now there have been discovered at Qumran (Caves 1 and 4) further Aramaic fragments of this older Testament of Levi,[2] two of which correspond to Test. Levi 14.1 ff.,[3] and also Hebrew fragments of a Testament of Naphtali, and of an Apocalypse of Jubilees (Cave 4) which has been used in the Greek Testament of Levi 14–17.[4] On the other hand, among the tens of thousands of fragments (in Cave 4 alone there are more than 25,000) of over 600 manuscripts which have been found in Qumran, none has been discovered which had to do with the remaining ten Testaments or supplied the text of the Greek versions of Levi and Naphtali.[5] Since a piece published in 1955 of a manuscript found in Cave 4 of the older Aramaic Testament of Levi was written approximately 100 BC,[6] we can affirm with certainty today that the Aramaic Testament of Levi originated at the latest in the second century BC, and the Greek version of the Testament of the Twelve Patriarchs not until considerably later, probably in Hellenistic Jewish circles.[7] Although matters are still uncertain, thanks to these discoveries we can see clearly enough to risk a cautious conjecture about the situation presupposed by the passage from Test. Levi 14.6 quoted above. This we venture to do on the strength of the participial clause, 'purifying them with unlawful purifications'. Its author opposes the introduction of proselyte baptism because he fears that it encourages mixed marriages, and he appeals to the fact that it lacks scriptural support ($\pi\alpha\rho\alpha\nu\acute{o}\mu\omega$). In fact we know that the adducing of scriptural authority for proselyte baptism, which was unknown to the Old Testament, gave many headaches to the Jewish theologians.[8] The participial phrase quoted above should therefore come from the time in which the assertion that

[1] R. H. Charles and A. Cowley, 'An Early Source of the Testaments of the Patriarchs', *JQR* 19, 1906/7, pp. 566–83 (Aramaic); W. Wright, *Catalogue of Syriac Manuscripts in the British Museum acquired since the Year 1838*, II, London, 1871, p. 997 (Syr.); R. H. Charles, *The Greek Versions of the Testaments of the Twelve Patriarchs*, 1908, pp. 245–56 (Aramaic, Syriac, Greek).
[2] D. Barthélemy and J. T. Milik, *Qumran Cave I* (Discoveries in the Judaean Desert I), Oxford, 1955, pp. 87–91; J. T. Milik, 'Le Testament de Lévi en araméen. Fragment de la grotte 4 de Qumrân', *RB* 62, 1955, pp. 398–406.
[3] Milik, 'Le Testament de Lévi', *op. cit.*, p. 399.
[4] Milik, reviewing de Jonge, *The Testaments of the Twelve Patriarchs*, *RB* 62, 1955, p. 298.
[5] Milik, *ibid.*
[6] Milik, 'Le Testament de Lévi', *op. cit.*, p. 399.
[7] This is supported, in my opinion, by the frequent personification of abstract concepts in the Greek Testaments of the Twelve Patriarchs which is also found in Paul.
[8] See below, pp. 31 f.

the Gentiles were Levitically impure was a contested novelty, i.e. from the end of the first century BC. If this conjecture be correct then we would have in Test. Levi 14.6 the hitherto missing direct proof that proselyte baptism was practised in pre-Christian times.

The rest of the evidence we can sum up briefly. Billerbeck, I 102–13, has said what is necessary about the oldest rabbinic reports about proselyte baptism, which are the next in time to appear. A discussion between the schools of Shammai and Hillel (both these teachers flourished in the last decades of the first century BC) presupposes proselyte baptism as a rite no longer in dispute,[1] and ascribes its beginning 'with certainty to pre-Christian times'.[2] Confirmation of this conclusion comes from St Paul, whose I Cor. 10.1 f. reveals a knowledge of a teaching maxim which obviously comes from the school of Rabbi Gamaliel I, with whom he studied in the third decade of our era. This maxim gave a biblical authority for proselyte baptism.[3] In addition to this it is very probable that the opinion of the Hillelites, who separated proselyte baptism by an interval of seven days from circumcision and thus made it the decisive act in joining the Jewish community,[4] had already carried the day in pre-New Testament times.[5] And lastly the manifold contacts between primitive Christian baptism and proselyte baptism show, as we have already mentioned, that the latter is the older, for it may be reckoned impossible that the rite did not originate until a time in which Christian baptism was already practised. Consequently the silence of Philo and Josephus must be judged accidental. In fact nearly all scholars who in the last sixty years have concerned themselves with the date of the introduction of proselyte

[1] Pes. 8.8 par. 'Eduy. 5.2; b. Pes. 92a. Tos. Pes. 7.13 (167), j. Pes. 8.36b. 47 f. and j. Naz. 8.57a. 48 f. adduce a concrete instance: 'There were in Jerusalem (Gentile) soldiers and watchers of ṣirin (the gates?) who (on 14th Nisan) took baptism and in the evening partook of the Passover Feast.' The author of the tradition is, according to the Erfurt manuscript of the Tosefta and according to j. Naz. 8.57a. 48 f., R. Eliezer ben Jacob the Elder (about 90), who is known to be specially reliable, according to j. Pes. 8.36b. 47, his son. The great antiquity of this report appears from the fact that it presupposes the dominance of the older Shammaite conception which ascribed to the Gentiles a lesser impurity than the Hillelite theory (about which see p. 25) and accordingly permitted the baptismal bath to be taken on the day of circumcision (see J. Jeremias, 'Proselytentaufe und Neues Testament', TZ 5, 1949, pp. 418–28). This instance could have been the occasion of the discussion reported in Pes. 8.8 between the Shammaites and the Hillelites.
[2] Billerbeck, I 103; his italics.
[3] See below, pp. 31 f.
[4] Billerbeck, I 104 f.
[5] The Hillelites justified the claim for a seven-day interval between circumcision and proselyte baptism by ascribing to the Gentiles the impurity pertaining to a corpse; statements of similar significance in the New Testament (John 18.28; cf. Matt. 8.8) and in Josephus, Ant. XVIII 4.3, § 94 (with reference to a date before AD 37), lead us to infer that already in New Testament times the dwellings of Gentiles living in Palestine were reckoned as being defiled by corpse-impurity (cf. Billerbeck, II 838 f.; Kel. 1.8).

baptism have come to the conclusion that it came into practice in pre-Christian times.[1]

B. *The connections between primitive Christian baptism and proselyte baptism*

Anyone who makes a close examination of proselyte baptism is astonished by the multiplicity of contacts with primitive Christian baptism. The first point to note is that the terminology of primitive Christian baptism shows the derivation of primitive Christian baptism from a Jewish background. That is true even of the verb 'to baptize' ($\beta\alpha\pi\tau\dot{\iota}\zeta\epsilon\iota\nu$) and its derivatives, which are nowhere used in non-Jewish Hellenism in a technical ritualistic sense;[2] these terms originate in the vocabulary of Greek-speaking Jews.[3] Moreover, the use of the middle voice, 'to dip oneself, wash oneself' ($\beta\alpha\pi\tau\dot{\iota}\zeta\epsilon\sigma\theta\alpha\iota$,[4] $\dot{\alpha}\pi o\lambda o\acute{\upsilon}\epsilon\sigma\theta\alpha\iota$[5]), is just as bad Greek[6] as it is good Jewish-Greek.[7] The use, also, of the preposition $\epsilon\dot{\iota}\varsigma$ $\tau\dot{o}$ $\ddot{o}\nu o\mu\alpha$ (for, with reference to) is typically Jewish baptismal terminology; it is a rendering of l^e *šem*, a formula by which, in rites of all kinds, the intention of the rite is introduced.[8]

If we consider now the administration of baptism, the resemblances in baptismal instruction are immediately obvious. The references to this in the New Testament are indeed only scanty and mostly indirect; but it is all the more significant that these few particulars have nearly all their corresponding parallels in the rite of proselyte baptism.

Not long ago the well-known rabbinist D. Daube submitted the 'Baptismal Catechism' handed down in b. Yeb. 47a.b (Bar.) to a pene-

---

[1] F. Weber, 1897; S. Krauss, 1902; A. Seeberg, 1905; E. Schürer, 1909; W. Brandt, 1910; H. L. Strack, 1911; G. Beer, 1912; I. Abrahams, 1917; P. Billerbeck, 1922; A. Oepke, 1928; F. Gavin, 1928; J. Leipoldt, 1928; H. H. Rowley, 1940; H. G. Marsh, 1941; E. Stauffer, 1941; F. J. Leenhardt, 1946; W. C. van Unnik, 1947; O. Cullmann, 1948; W. F. Flemington, 1948; W. Michaelis, 1949; T. W. Manson, 1949; H. Sahlin, 1949; T. F. Torrance, 1954; D. Daube, 1956; W. Foerster, 1956; B. Neunheuser, 1956.
[2] A. Oepke, $\beta\dot{\alpha}\pi\tau\omega$ $\kappa.\tau.\lambda.$, *TWNT* I, p. 530, 8–10.
[3] LXX 4. *Baσ.* 5.14; Sir. 34 [31]. 25; Judith 12.7.
[4] I Cor. 10.2 (P[46] B ç al Or, early changed into the passive); Acts 22.16.
[5] I Cor. 6.11.
[6] J. Leipoldt, 'Die altchristliche Taufe religionsgeschichtlich betrachtet', *WZU Leipzig* 3, 1953/54, p. 65.
[7] Judith 12.7: $\dot{\epsilon}\beta\alpha\pi\tau\dot{\iota}\zeta\epsilon\tau o$. This middle is a rendering of the Hebrew *ṭabhal*, Aramaic *t^ebhal*, which in the Qal has the meaning 'to take the baptismal bath', 'to dip oneself'.
[8] The phrase $\beta\alpha\pi\tau\dot{\iota}\zeta\epsilon\iota\nu$ $\epsilon\dot{\iota}\varsigma$ $\tau\dot{o}$ $\ddot{o}\nu o\mu\alpha$ has nothing to do with the usage of Hellenistic banking terminology, in which $\epsilon\dot{\iota}\varsigma$ $\tau\dot{o}$ $\ddot{o}\nu o\mu\alpha$ means 'on the account of' (so recently A. Oepke, *op. cit.*, p. 537). Rather is $\epsilon\dot{\iota}\varsigma$ $\tau\dot{o}$ $\ddot{o}\nu o\mu\alpha$, as the variant translations $\dot{\epsilon}\pi\dot{\iota}$ $\tau\tilde{\omega}$ $\dot{o}\nu\dot{o}\mu\alpha\tau\iota$ (Acts 2.38) and $\dot{\epsilon}\nu$ $\tau\tilde{\omega}$ $\dot{o}\nu\dot{o}\mu\alpha\tau\iota$ (Acts 10.48) show, a translation of the prefix l^e *šum*, l^e *šem* 'for', 'with reference to', with which in rabbinic literature the intention purposed in a cultic action like sacrifice, baptismal bath, etc. is introduced (Billerbeck, I 1054 f.; IV 744).

trating analysis.[1] Following the sequence of the text he finds a 'pattern of instruction' with five subdivisions: (a) testing of the motives for change of religion; (b) instruction about the Commandments; (c) on the duty of charity; (d) on penalties; (e) on rewards and the world to come. The primitive Church seems, if we can trust Acts 2.37-42, not to have had at the very beginning an independent course of baptismal instruction —understandably enough, since the Jews who joined themselves to the fellowship remained at first in the community of the synagogue and only distinguished themselves from their co-religionists by their acknowledgement of Jesus as the Messiah. But very soon, at the latest when Christianity moved out into the Gentile world, the necessity of a course of baptismal instruction must have arisen. Certainly it would appear that Daube goes too far when, basing himself on characteristics noticed in the catechetical style (e.g. the use of the participle to express a command[2]), on the vocabulary and on the illustrative material of the New Testament, he concludes 'On the whole, then, the Jewish scheme was taken over'.[3] We have, in my opinion, too little certain information about the catechumenate in preparation for baptism in the primitive Christian Church to give so decisive a judgment. But it is possible to say that the contacts between Jewish and Christian instruction of catechumens were close. For it is very probable that the primitive Church also inquired whether there were any obstacle for admission to baptism, as we shall later see.[4] Didache 7.1 informs us[5] that a course of moral instruction preceded baptism, a course expounded by the 'Two Ways Scheme' (Did. 1–6), and we may conjecture from the First Epistle of Peter[6] that the injunction to charity had a dominating position in primitive Christian baptismal instruction, even if we do not see in this letter the working-over of a baptismal address or indeed of a baptismal liturgy, but explain the numerous echoes of baptismal terminology by the theory that the letter was addressed to the new converts of a recently completed great missionary drive.[7] And, lastly we learn with certainty from Heb. 6.2 that the eschatological punishments and the eschatological retribution as well as the world to come were themes that belonged to the instruction preparatory to primitive Christian baptism. Indeed this important verse enumerates

---

[1] D. Daube, The New Testament and Rabbinic Judaism (Jordan Lectures in Comparative Religion 2), London, 1956, pp. 106-40 ('A Baptismal Catechism').
[2] Cf. op. cit., p. 102.
[3] Op. cit., p. 125.
[4] See below, pp. 53 f.
[5] Cf. Leipoldt, op. cit., p. 63.
[6] 1.22 f.; 2.17; 3.8-12; 4.7b-9.
[7] Cf. the enumeration of the provinces in I Peter 1.1.

the four most important items of primitive Christian baptismal instruction, as it was handled in the church of those to whom the letter was addressed, and among them 'Resurrection of the dead and eternal judgment'.

Even clearer than these contacts between primitive Christian baptismal instruction and the catechumenate of proselytes are the correspondences in the external administration of baptism. Here as there baptism is by complete immersion;[1] here as there flowing water is preferred, but not regarded as unconditionally necessary;[2] here as there, at least in some districts, the baptized person makes a confession of sins on the occasion of his baptism.[3] Especially significant is the discovery that Christian baptism and proselyte baptism were identical even in such technical details as the regulation that before baptism women should let down their hair and take off their ornaments.[4]

To these contacts between primitive Christian baptism and proselyte baptism in the matter of terminology, of baptismal instruction and the baptismal rite must be added in conclusion the following correspondences in the doctrine of baptism and its illustrative material.

The introduction of proselyte baptism was not, as we have seen,[5] achieved without opposition. The objection was made to it that it lacked scriptural authority. And in fact there was nowhere in the Old Testament a passage which enjoined that the Gentile who changed his religion should be baptized. Old rabbinic discussions[6] show us what difficulty the

---

[1] Christian: Rom. 6.4 (συνετάφημεν); Col. 2.12 (συνταφέντες); cf. further the middle I Cor. 6.11 (ἀπελούσασθε); Acts 22.16 (βάπτισαι); I Cor. 10.2 according to the better reading (ἐβαπτίσαντο P⁴⁶B ς al Or); Ps.-Clem. Hom. 9.23.2 (βαπτισάμενοι). The objections of E. Stommel, ' "Begraben mit Christus" (Rom. 6.4) und der Taufritus', Römische Quartalschrift für christliche Altertumskunde und Kirchengeschichte 49, 1954, pp. 1–20, have not convinced me; the shallowness of the piscinas of the West proves, in my opinion, only that there was an early departure from immersion. Rabbinic: Immersion, inclusive of the head: b. 'Erub. 4b; b. B.Q. 82 a, b (cf. n. 4 below and I. Abrahams, 'How did the Jews baptize?', JTS 12, 1910/11. pp. 609–12).

[2] Christian baptism: Did. 7.1–3. Proselyte baptism: Billerbeck, I 108 f. under III–IV; Orac. Sib. IV 165 (see below, p. 34). Leipoldt rightly emphasizes, op. cit., p. 64, that the interest in such external matters is by itself enough to indicate Jewish influence.

[3] Christian: I Peter 3.21 (according to the most probable translation: 'Pray for a good conscience'); Aristides of Athens, Apol. 17.4 (see below, p. 71). Jewish: Orac. Sib. IV 165–70 (see below, p. 34); Qoh. r. on 1.8 (see below, pp. 33 f., n. 10).

[4] Christian: Hippolytus: Apostolic Tradition 21.5 (Egyptian Church Order 16.6; Coptic Can. 46, Till-Leipoldt 19; Arabic Can. 34, Périer-Périer 603 [53]; Ethiopic Can. 34, Duensing 55); Test. Dom. II 8 (Rahmani 126); Can. Hippol. 19.7 (Riedel 211). The Latin text for this passage has not been preserved. Rabbinic: b. B. Q. 82a, b. Cf. W. C. van Unnik's excellent investigation, 'Les cheveux défaits des femmes baptisées. Un rite de baptême dans l'Ordre Ecclésiastique d'Hippolyte', Vigiliae Christianae I, 1947, pp. 77–100, in which he convincingly proved the dependence of this Christian baptismal regulation on the rite of proselyte baptism.

[5] See above, pp. 26–28, on Test. Levi 14.6.

[6] They have been reproduced by me in full in 'Der Ursprung der Johannestaufe', ZNW 28, 1929, pp. 316–18.

Hillelite scribes had in providing the missing scriptural authority. The device employed was to start with Num. 15.14 'as ye do, so shall he (the stranger) do'. This sentence the Hillelites interpreted to mean that the proselyte should be received within the Sinaitic Covenant as the people of Israel once were at Sinai.[1] Thus they made the assumption that the people of Israel at Sinai had been baptized before their reception into the Covenant. There is indeed no mention of this in the Book of Exodus. But this act of baptism was inferred from Ex. 24.8 where it is written 'Moses took blood and sprinkled the people therewith' for 'It is valid traditional teaching that there is no sprinkling without (previous) baptism'.[2] Thus scriptural proof was adduced for proselyte baptism.[3] In this way originated the doctrine of the baptism of the generation of the desert wandering before the reception of salvation at Sinai. I Cor. 10.1–2 shows us that this doctrine of the baptism of the desert generation, which is of fundamental importance for proselyte baptism, was already familiar to Paul, the pupil of the Hillelite Gamaliel I.[4] He applied it to Christian baptism: as the Jewish theologians saw in this baptism of the desert generation the exemplar of proselyte baptism, so Paul saw in it the type of Christian baptism.

We turn now to a second fundamental doctrine of Jewish conversion theology. The theological interpretation of change of religion is formulated in the often-quoted proposition 'The proselyte in his conversion (to Judaism) is like a newborn child.'[5] This comparison (early interpreted in a juristic sense) of the proselyte to a newborn child had originally a purely religious meaning,[6] and signified that the conversion to Judaism

---

[1] b. Ker. 9a, par. 81a, cited *op. cit.*, pp. 316 f.
[2] b. Yeb. 46b; further in b. Ker. 9a, par. 81a. An attempt to infer from Ex. 19.10 that baptism was practised in the generation of the desert wandering before the sealing of the Covenant is rejected in Yeb. 46b because this might mean a profane baptism; cf. *op. cit.*, p. 318.
[3] At least for the Hillelites. The Shammaites rejected this reasoning (b. Yeb. 46a: R. Eliezer ben Hyrcanus).
[4] A. Merx, *Das Evangelium Matthaeus nach der syrischen im Sinaikloster gefundenen Palimpsesthandschrift* (Die vier kanonischen Evangelien nach ihrem ältesten bekannten Texte II 1), Berlin, 1902, pp. 40 f.; J. Jeremias, 'Der Ursprung der Johannestaufe', *ZNW* 28, 1929, pp. 312–20; H. Sahlin, *Studien zum dritten Kapitel des Lukasevangeliums* (Uppsala Universitets Årsskrift 2), 1949, p. 113.
[5] b. Yeb. 48b (Bar.) par. Ger. 2.6 f.; further b. Yeb. 22a, 62a, 97b; b. Bek. 47a.
[6] Billerbeck, II 423; G. F. Moore, *Judaism in the First Centuries of the Christian Era* I, Cambridge (Mass.), 1927, pp. 334 f.; J. Jeremias, *Jerusalem zur Zeit Jesu* II B2, Göttingen, 1937 = ²1958, pp. 196 f.; H. Sahlin, *op. cit.*, pp. 115 f. The juristic interpretation of the sentence, that the Gentile who changes his religion is in legal matters (e.g. in matters pertaining to the law of marriage) to be regarded as a new creation, namely, 'without father and mother and (other) relations' (Rashi on b. Sanh. 57b. Bar.), is secondary (compare J. Jeremias, *ibid.*).

gave rise to a wholly new life, a new creation.[1] How old this doctrine is can be seen from the fact that as early as in the pre-Christian Jewish-Hellenistic propaganda tract *Joseph and Asenath* the promise is made to Asenath as she joins the Jewish community: 'You will be renewed and recreated and will receive new life' (ἀνακαινισθῇσῃ καὶ ἀναπλασθῇσῃ καὶ ἀναζωοποιηθῇσῃ);[2] her conversion thus signifies renewal, new creation, restoration to life. This thought occurs again in the oldest rabbinic utterance about proselyte baptism Pes. 8.8.[3] In this passage the Hillelites justify their claim that the proselyte must not be baptized till seven days after circumcision with the strange proposition 'He who separates himself from his foreskin, separates as it were from the grave (*qebher*)!' This phrase, which as a description of the removal of Levitical impurity is quite without analogy, had likewise at first a purely religious sense and signified that the proselyte was as one who rose from the grave or (since *qebher* also signifies the mother's womb) as one who had just been born.[4] The change of religion is thus 'a passage from death to life',[5] a resurrection from the dead or a new birth. Correspondingly it is stated that the proselytes are men who have risen from the dead,[6] and we meet with *Nyptyys* (=νεόφυτος) 'the newborn' as the name of a proselyte.[7] This new creation resulted from '*all his sins being forgiven* him (the proselyte) (on his conversion) (by God)'.[8] The date of this dogma can be ascertained from the fact that as early as the first century BC we are told that Asenath's admission to Judaism was prefaced by a confession of sins.[9] The Midrash gives us a concrete example of the connection of the admission ceremony to Judaism with a confession of sins.[10] Extra-rabbinic evidence dated

---

[1] Gen. r. 39 (near the end) on 12.5: 'Everyone who brings a Gentile near (makes him a proselyte) is as if he had created him'; Cant. r. 1 on 1.3: 'He who brings a creature under the pinions of the Šᵉ khina, to him is given credit, as if he had created, shaped and formed him.'

[2] 15 (ed. P. Batiffol, *Le livre de la Prière d'Aseneth* [Studia Patristica 1–2], Paris, 1889–90, p. 61.5). The pre-Christian date of the writing is evident especially from the fact that it knows nothing of proselyte baptism, cf. G. D. Kilpatrick, 'The Last Supper', *ExpT* 64, 1952/3, pp. 4–8, here see pp. 4 f.; J. Jeremias, 'Die missionarische Aufgabe in der Mischehe (I Cor. 7.16)', in *Neutestamentliche Studien für Rudolf Bultmann*, p. 255–60. On the propaganda character of the writing: J. Jeremias, *Jesus' Promise to the Nations*, ET (SBT 24), London, 1958, pp. 12 f.

[3] On the early date of the passage see above, p. 28 n. 1.

[4] E. Baneth in *Mischnaioth* II, Berlin, 1920, p. 227 n. 56; Daube, *The New Testament and Rabbinic Judaism*, p. 110.

[5] Daube, *ibid.*

[6] Qoh. r. on 8.10 (ed. Stettin, 1864, 112a).

[7] b. Yeb. 98a; cf. B. J. Bamberger, *Proselytism in the Talmudic Period*, Cincinnati, 1939, pp. 245, 264.

[8] j. Bik. 3.65c. 61; Midr. Sam. 17 § 1 on 13.1; cf. b. Yeb. 48b (Bar.) par. Ger. 2.6 (Billerbeck, II 423).

[9] *Joseph and Asenath*, 12 f.

[10] Qoh. r. on 1.8 (ed. Stettin, 70a. 30–70b. 5): 'An incident with a woman who came

C

about AD 80 for the mediation of forgiveness through baptism is provided by *Orac. Sib.* IV. 162 ff.:

> 165 'Bathe the whole body in ever-flowing streams[1]
> 166 And reach your hands to heaven, praying forgiveness
> 167 For these things that ye have done.'[2]

All these statements about the effects of conversion to Judaism are summarized briefly in the frequently used formula, that the proselyte from the day of his baptism onwards is in a state of holiness (*biqᵉ-dhuśśa*).[3]

How powerfully the thought that conversion signified the beginning of a completely new life had penetrated the consciousness of the great mass of the people, is proved by the numerous instances in inscriptions and literary sources of *changes of name of proselytes*. This usage goes far back into the centuries before the introduction of proselyte baptism. The oldest evidence comes from Egypt; in a Jewish-Aramaic document from

to R. Eliezer (about AD 90) in order to change over to Jewish religion (*lhtgyyr*). She spoke to him: "Rabbi, bring me near!" He said to her, "Recount thy deeds!" She said, "My youngest son (is the child) of my eldest son." He cried out against her. She went to R. Joshua (about AD 90) and he accepted her. Then said his disciples to him, "Rabbi E. rejects her and will you accept her?" He said to them, "Now that she has decided to become a Jew, *'ynh ḥyh l'wlm*, she will not live at all (much longer)", cf. Prov. 2.19: "None that go unto her return again", and if they turn back, "neither take they hold of the paths of life".' Here it is unambiguously stated that before admission a confession of sins is required—'Recount thy deeds.' Admittedly this confession, according to the text before us, does not bring forgiveness with it, but it is expected that the woman will die soon after changing her religion. But it is questionable whether the concluding Scripture quotation is original, for the harlot in Prov. 2.19 ('none that go unto her') is taken (e.g. 'Aboda Zara 17a) to refer to heresy, so that a contradiction arises: the beginning of the text sees in the woman a Gentile who becomes a Jew, the end a repentant heretic. If one disregards the secondary Scripture quotation, then the words *'ynh ḥyh l'wlm* signify 'then she does not live any more'—i.e she is regarded as if she had not lived before at all (A. Wünsche, *Der Midrasch Kohelet* [Bibliotheca Rabbinica 1], Leipzig, 1880, p. 163). Daube also understands the passage thus, *The New Testament and Rabbinic Judaism*, p. 113 n. 1, since he cites our passage as a proof that, on changing his religion, the proselyte's sins are forgiven. (Unfortunately the parallel passage b. 'Aboda Zara 17a does not take us any further. It runs, 'A woman came before Rab Ḥisda [died AD 309] and said to him that the least of the little she had done was that her youngest son was the son of her eldest. And Rab Ḥisda said in respect of her, "Get ready her burial shroud." But she did not die.')

[1] Cf. Acts 16.13.
[2] The aorist imperative λούσασθε (line 165) shows that the reference is to a unique bathing, therefore the passage cannot refer to the washings of the Jewish baptist sects. The following also refer the passage to proselyte baptism: E. Schürer, *Geschichte des jüdischen Volkes im Zeitalter Jesu Christi* III⁴, Leipzig, 1909, p. 173; J. Leipoldt, *Die urchristliche Taufe im Lichte der Religionsgeschichte*, Leipzig, 1928, pp. 18 f.; F. M. Derwacter, *Preparing the Way for Paul: the Proselyte Movement in Later Judaism*, New York, 1930, p. 106; Oepke, 'βάπτω', *TWNT* I, p. 533; W. F. Flemington, *The New Testament Doctrine of Baptism*, London, 1948, p. 5.
[3] References: see below, p. 46 n. 4.

Aswan of the year 420 BC an Egyptian of the name of As-Hor appears, who four years later, 416 BC, is called Nathan; obviously in the interval he had been converted to Judaism.[1] In the writing mentioned above, *Joseph and Asenath* (first century before Christ), we read in ch. 15, 'You shall no longer be called Asenath, but your name shall be "City of Refuge".'

To the period before AD 70 belongs a Jerusalem inscription concerning the proselyte Mryh;[2] since Maria is a Jewish name, it is probable that the woman took it on changing her religion. The same is true of the Ammonite proselyte Yehuda (about AD 90)[3] and the Egyptian proselyte Binyamin.[4] The epitaph (third century AD) of a certain Beturia (=Veturia) Paucla, aged 86, who was converted to Judaism at the age of 70, reads: *proselita an(nos) XVI nominae Sara* (lines 6 f.);[5] the old lady thus called herself Sara for the last 16 years of her life. The rabbinic evidence fills out the picture. Repeatedly in the Talmud a Rab Isaac bar Jacob bar *giore* (the son of the proselytes) is mentioned.[6] From the plural *giore* we conclude that both parents of this scribe were proselytes; the father certainly adopted the Jewish name Jacob on his conversion. The same holds in the case of Rab Shemu'el bar Yehuda (about 300) who refused to take part in a trial at which the Ḥaliṣa[7] was to take place, on the grounds that he was a proselyte;[8] his father too will not have brought his Jewish name Yehuda out of his Gentile past. The usage of changing one's name is even used to help in the interpretation of Scripture. Commenting on Gen. 14.14, 'Abraham . . . armed his trained servants (*ḥanikhaw*)', the Midrash remarks '*ḥanikhaw* means "men of his name (*ḥanikhatho*)". They were called Abraham like him.'[9] Since the 'trained servants' refers to Abraham's slaves, the Midrash assumes, with the help of a pun, that Abraham converted them, and since their change of religion they bore his name. The documents show that the proselytes had

---

[1] E. Schürer, *op. cit.*, III⁴, pp. 29, 185.

[2] S. Klein, *Jüdisch-palästinisches Corpus Inscriptionum*, Vienna and Berlin, 1920, pp. 24 f., no. 50; *CII* II 321 f., no. 1390.

[3] Yad. 4.4; Tos. Yad. 2.17 f. (683); b. Ber. 28a (Bar.).

[4] Tos. Qid. 5.4 (342). On the form of the name Minjamin which the Erfurt MS gives, cf. R. de Vaux, 'Binjamin-Minjamin', *RB* 45 (1936), pp. 400 2; Jeremias, *Jerusalem zur Zeit Jesu* II B 2, p. 194 n. 50.

[5] *CII* I 383 f., no. 523; cf. E. Diehl, *Lateinische altchristliche Inschriften* (Kleine Texte 26-28)², Bonn, 1913, p. 62, no. 363; *ILCV* II 4897. The inscription *CII* I 340 f., no. 462, surely does not belong to this group.

[6] b. 'Erub. 62a; b. M. Q. 18a end; b. Keth. 46a end; b. Ḥull. 101b, cf. b. Ta'an. 29b.

[7] The taking off of one's shoe as a sign of refusal of levirate marriage.

[8] b. Yeb. 101b.

[9] Gen. r. 43.2 on 14.14 (ed. Stettin, 88a. 15).

a predilection for choosing the names of the patriarchs and matriarchs.

It is particularly instructive with the New Testament in mind once more to place together the different phrases and images which are used to describe the result of change of religion which was effected in the case of male persons by circumcision and baptism, in the case of females by baptism alone. We note in each case the New Testament parallels.

The Gentile who changes his religion, who previously was far from God, has now come near to him (see p. 33 note 1; cf. Eph. 2.13; Acts 2.39). He was dead (see above, pp. 32 f.; cf. Eph. 2.1), lay, in a manner of speaking, in the grave (see above, p. 33; cf. I Clem. 38.3) and has been raised from the dead (ibid.; cf. Col. 3.1 among other passages). A new creation has taken place (see above, p. 33, 'You will be renewed and recreated and will receive new life'; cf. Gal. 6.15; II Cor. 5.17). Thereby his past is blotted out, he has entered into a completely new existence, is like a newborn child (see above, pp. 32 f.; cf. I Pet. 2.2), is a νεόφυτος (see above, p. 33; cf. I Tim. 3.6).[1] All this happened through forgiveness of all his sins being granted to the Gentile on his change of religion (see above, pp. 33 f.; cf. Col. 2 and frequently). Henceforth he is in holiness (biqᵉdhuššaʾ, see above, p. 34;[2] cf. I. Thess. 3.13).

It is worthy of notice that in these correspondences we have not merely individual points of contact, but that the whole terminology of the Jewish conversion theology connected with proselyte baptism recurs in the theology of primitive Christian baptism. Here a chance coincidence and the possibility of accidental analogies is wholly inconceivable; the only possible conclusion is that the rites are related as parent and child. The problem to which this conclusion gives rise has hardly been noticed hitherto, but does not concern us here.[3] We note only the following fact:

[1] Cf. E. Sjöberg, 'Wiedergeburt und Neuschöpfung im palästinischen Judentum', ST 4, 1950, pp. 44–85; 'Neuschöpfung in den Toten-Meer-Rollen', ST 9, 1955, pp. 131–36.

[2] For further references see below, p. 46 n. 4.

[3] This only may be noted, that much more reserve of judgment will have to be exercised in ascribing an early date to Hellenistic influences on Christian baptismal doctrine and practice than is common now. Since I Cor. 15.29 is cited as the most striking evidence of Hellenistic influence on the baptismal practice in the Pauline churches, it may be mentioned that the interpretation of this passage as referring to a vicarious baptism for persons who died unbaptized has, in my opinion, been refuted. M. Raeder, 'Vikariatstaufe in 1 Cor. 15.29?', ZNW 46, 1955, pp. 258–60, has convincingly shown that in the phrase 'ἐπεὶ τί ποιήσουσιν οἱ βαπτιζόμενοι ὑπὲρ τῶν νεκρῶν' (a) the ὑπέρ has a final sense ('for the sake of so-and-so'), and (b) the term οἱ νεκροί refers to dead Christians. We must accordingly translate 'What then are those people to do, who submit to baptism for the sake of the dead (i.e. in order to be reunited in the resurrection with their dead relatives or friends who have received Christian baptism)?' (p. 260). Take, for instance, a case in which a young woman belonging to the Church, and engaged to be married, died, and whose heathen bridegroom had himself baptized 'for her sake'—that is, in order to be united with her

true though it be that Christian baptism, as baptism in the name of the Messiah Jesus and as impartation of a share in his kingly rule, is fundamentally different from proselyte baptism, yet it must also be affirmed that the scheme of instruction for primitive Christian baptism, the primitive Christian rite and its theological terminology are to a great extent imported from the realm of proselyte baptism.

Now we must take into account the fact that especially in the East rites persist tenaciously even when their significance and interpretation alter. Accordingly when we seek clarification of the question whether the primitive Church baptized children as well as adults when they changed their religion, we shall have to give all the more weight to the corresponding procedure in relation to proselyte baptism.

C. The administration of proselyte baptism to children

What was the procedure in proselyte baptism? Was it administered to children? The answer is that when Gentiles adopted the Jewish faith it was completely taken for granted that at the same time the children also, including even very young children,[1] should be received into the Jewish faith,[2] The oldest rabbinic sources, the Tannaitic traditions, give numerous instances of the reception of small Gentile children and babies into the Jewish faith. That here we have a certain amount of information we owe to the circumstance that in these cases certain legal questions arose which varied according to the sex of the child concerned. In the case of the reception of Gentile *boys*, the all-important thing was to determine the date of circumcision. About this a Tannaitic rule lays down, 'If anyone buys a pregnant (Gentile) slave and she gives birth thereafter (to a boy), then that is a (slave-child, cf. Gen. 17.12) bought with money, to be circumcised *on the eighth* (day); but if anyone buys a (Gentile) slave and her child with her, that is a (slave-child) bought with money

in the resurrection. This interpretation fits excellently into the context of the apologetic reflections of I Cor. 15.12–19, which Paul, after the digression of vv. 20–28, resumes in vv. 29–34. The apostle had said in v. 18 that if Christ were not risen 'they who are fallen asleep in Christ are perished'. Now he adds that the same is true of their Gentile kinsmen (husbands, wives, lovers), who had themselves baptized in order to be united with them in the resurrection. Cf. J. Jeremias, ' "Flesh and Blood cannot inherit the Kingdom of God" (I Cor. XV 50)', *NTS* 2, 1955/56, pp. 151–59, here pp. 155 f. If this interpretation is correct, then 'vicarious baptism' is to be deleted from the vocabulary of New Testament exegesis. The superstitious misuse of representative baptism for the dead, which was practised in heretical circles since the end of the second century, did not arise about AD 50 in Corinth, only to be tolerated in silence by Paul, but arose from a gross misunderstanding of the (certainly very telegraphic) formulation of I Cor. 15.29.

[1] Billerbeck, I 110–12.
[2] Sons: Yeb. 11.2; Tos. Yeb. 12.2 (254); Tos. Bekh. 6.3 (540); b. Shab. 135a, 135b (Bar.). Daughters: Keth. 4.3. Children: Sheb. 10.9; b. Keth. 11a.

to be circumcised[1,2] *on the first* (day).' The circumcision of the slave-child thus followed normally on the eighth day after birth; but if mother and child were sold, then the circumcision must take place at once on the first day,[3] and it made no difference whether the mother and child were left together or separated.[4] An analogous distinction in relation to the day of circumcision holds also for the Gentile boy born in freedom: 'A (male) proselyte (child) is under certain circumstances circumcised on the eighth day. What do "certain circumstances" mean? If the boy was born *before* the baptism of his mother, then he is circumcised on the first day.[5] If he was born *after* the baptism of his mother, he is circumcised on the eighth day.'[6] That means, then, that while the Jewish boy is invariably circumcised on the eighth day, the Gentile infant in certain cases (if the mother was not yet baptized at the birth of her child) was circumcised *as soon as the day of birth*.[7] In the case of girls the question arose whether in relation to certain regulations of marriage law they were considered on a par with Jewish girls. The frequently repeated decision ran thus: the age of three years constitutes a limit.[8] Gentile girls who at the moment of change of religion were younger than three years and one day (*šennithgayyᵉru . . . pᵉḥuthoth mibbᵉnoth šaloš šanim wᵉyom 'eḥadh*), are considered on a par with Jewish girls.[9] Since in the case of girls, baptism was the only act of admission, these passages indirectly prove for the Tannaitic period the baptism of Gentile girls at the earliest age; in fact the term *nithgayyer* includes the baptismal bath as early as the beginning of the first century AD (Pes. 8.8.)[10] The first *direct mention* of the baptism of young proselyte children is by Rab Huna (*c.* 212–297) who describes the procedure at the admission of a young proselyte child whose father had died: 'He was directed to take the baptismal bath on the grounds of a decision of the court of justice.'[11]

---

[1] b. Shab. 135b (Bar.). Thus, for the sake of casuistry, the case is considered that a Gentile slave is sold by a Gentile owner to a Jew on the same day on which she had borne a son.

[2] In the context the first day means the day of the birth, not the day of the purchase (so Billerbeck, IV 724).

[3] See previous note.   [4] b. Shab. 135b.

[5] The phrase used here, *ben yomo*, recurs a few lines later (Ger. 2.6) and means there unambiguously a newly-born child.

[6] Ger. 2.1.

[7] The Tannaitic rule b. Shab. 135b (Bar.) speaks unambiguously of the circumcision of a Gentile slave-child on the day of birth: 'There are (slave-children, cf. Gen. 17.12) born in the house who are to be circumcised on the first day.'

[8] This limiting age is connected with views about virginity (cf. Nid. 5.4 end).

[9] Keth. 1. 2,4; 3. 1,2; b. Qid. 78a (Bar.) par. b. Yeb. 60b; j. Qid. 4. 66a. 10; j. Bik. 1. 64a. 31f.; j. Yeb. 8. 9b. 62f.

[10] For the date, see above, p. 28 n. 1.

[11] b. Keth. 11a, cf. Billerbeck, I 112.

The next witness is Rab Huna's pupil 'Abba, who was one of the orators at the funeral ceremony of his teacher in the year 297: 'R. Hezekiah (taught) in the name of R. Ba (= 'Abba):[1] that is so (as) if he had found a foundling child in his midst (the midst of the land of Israel?); if he had it *dipped* in the name of a slave, then thou must circumcise it in the name of a slave; if in the name of a free man, then thou must circumcise it in the name of a free man.'[2] The foundling child receives a baptismal bath because it is possibly a Gentile child. There follows an utterance of Raba (299–352): 'If a non-Israelite during her pregnancy becomes a proselyte, then her child does not need the baptismal bath.'[3] The passage shows that if the birth occurred *before the baptism* of the mother, the infant was baptized along with the mother on her admission. Lastly we have to mention also the decision handed down from the fourth century AD that sons and daughters of Gentiles who as minors were received into the Jewish faith along with their parents, could reverse the step when they had attained their majority.[4] We see that the oldest rabbinic sources take it completely for granted that the children, even the smallest children, were admitted with their parents into the Jewish faith; the case is nowhere mentioned, and is almost inconceivable for the feeling of the times, where on the admission of both parents the children who were minors remained Gentiles. For the girls the act of admission was baptism, for the boys it was preceded by circumcision, which, as we saw,[5] in certain circumstances had to be administered as early as the day of birth.

In view of the close connections between primitive Christian baptism and proselyte baptism, which on pp. 29–37 we established not only in respect of baptismal terminology and the illustrative material used in interpretation of baptism, but also in reference to the external ritual of baptism right down to details (letting down the hair and laying aside of ornaments in the case of women, p. 31), it must be assumed that in the question of infant baptism also the Christian baptismal ritual corresponded to that of proselyte baptism, i.e. that with the admission of Gentiles to Christianity children of every age, including infants, were baptized also.

Col. 2.11 adds confirmation of this point. Paul here names baptism 'the Christian circumcision' (ἡ περιτομὴ τοῦ Χριστοῦ) and describes it

---

[1] W. Bacher, *Tradition und Tradenten in den Schulen Palästinas und Babyloniens*, Leipzig, 1914, p. 407 n. 12.
[2] j. Yeb. 8. 8d. 45–47.
[3] b. Yeb. 78a.
[4] b. Keth. 11a: Rab Joseph (died 333); Billerbeck is I 112.
[5] See above, p. 38.

thereby as the Christian sacrament which corresponds to Jewish circumcision and replaces it; he has earlier, in II Cor. 1.22 (cf. Eph. 1.13; 4.30) transferred the description of circumcision as a 'seal' (Rom. 4.11) to baptism. Circumcision was, however, administered on the admission of a Gentile household to the Jewish faith to all male members of the household, even to infants from eight days after birth upwards. The description of baptism as 'Christian circumcision' makes it very probable that the procedure in baptism was the same, that is, that children of every age were baptized along with their parents when the latter were converted to the Christian faith.

3. INDIVIDUAL PIECES OF EVIDENCE

Only against the background disclosed by our investigation of the *oikos* formula and the practice of proselyte baptism can the individual pieces of evidence for the practice of child baptism at the admission of parents be justly assessed.

Let us begin with the Jewish Christian Church. Here we must first cite Acts 2.38 f. After the Pentecost sermon Peter says: 'Repent, and be baptized every one of you in the name of Jesus Christ for the forgiveness of your sins: and you shall receive the gift of the Holy Spirit. For the promise is to you and to your children and to all that are far off, every one whom the Lord our God calls to him.' Who are the 'children' (τέκνα) mentioned in v. 39? Are their descendants meant? In view of the immediate expectation of the End, which did not reckon with coming generations, this interpretation of words spoken in the very earliest days of the Church has nothing to recommend it, but could be conceivable for the time of Luke. And yet the context speaks against it. The 'promise' of which v. 39 says that it is valid also for the children, is in fact the promise of Joel which was mentioned in 2.17–21, the promise, namely, that God will pour out his Spirit upon all flesh and that 'Your sons and daughters will prophesy' (Acts 2.17=Joel 2.28). The promise of the Spirit is for the children just as for 'your young men' and 'your old men' (*ibid*). Thus the children are not coming generations, but the sons and daughters of the hearers. Since the gift of the Spirit (2.38) is linked to baptism, 2.39 contains the challenge to have the children baptized also. Thus in Acts 2.38 f. we have before us a witness for the practice of infant baptism in apostolic times, at any rate in the time of the composition of Luke's twofold work: that is to say, for the baptism of children of Jewish parents on their admission into the Christian Church. This is consonant with the fact that among the baptized 'households' mentioned in Acts and by Paul at least one Jewish household is named, and perhaps a second.[1] At the most one can ask if in Acts 2.38 f. an age-limit is indirectly presupposed. H. Windisch reckoned that here older children must be thought of, namely such as are ripe for the repentance mentioned in 2.38 and can prophesy (2.17).[2] This limitation is however highly improbable because the salvation from the final judgment mediated by baptism (2.40; cf. 2.21) excludes any limitation of age.

Let us turn to the Gentile Christian Church. Here voices from the most widely scattered territories bear us unanimous witness that the primitive usage of baptizing households (Acts 11.14; 16.15, 33; 18.8; cf. I Cor. 1.16)[3] survived uniformly in east and west. Hippolytus graphically describes to us how in the Roman Church long before his time, as early as the second century, at the festival of Easter the families who were being admitted were baptized; first the children, including the infants who could not yet speak (i.e. answer the baptismal questions), then the adult males and last the women (see pp. 74 f.). Tertullian also takes us into the second century, but to Africa. He is the first to report to us the custom that godparents (*sponsores*) took part in the baptismal ceremony who made promises for the future Christian 'walk and conversation' of the infants (*parvuli*, see pp. 81–84); they are most probably identical with the sponsors mentioned in the Church Orders, who stood surety for those intending to change their religion when names of candidates for the catechumenate were announced, and in this character vouched for the families of the infants. And lastly we are pointed to Syria by the Pseudo-Clementine writings, which at least indirectly bear witness that families were not torn asunder at baptism (see pp. 68 f.). All these records will be considered in detail in their place in Chapter 3.

The inscriptions on children's tombstones of the early period unfortunately inform us only in very exceptional cases what the confessional standing of the parents was. But we have at least one inscription of the third century,[4] which more informative than the rest, lets us know that it is relevant to our context here. It reports an occurrence which quite certainly was not unique:

d(is) m(anibus) s(acrum)
Florentius filio suo Aproniano

---

[1] Acts 18.8; and perhaps also I Cor. 1.16, see above, pp. 19 f.
[2] 'Zum Problem der Kindertaufe im Urchristentum', *ZNW* 28, 1929, p. 123.
[3] We do not know for certain whether Stephanas was a Jewish or a Gentile Christian.
[4] I owe this dating to the kindness of A. M. Schneider.

fecit titulum benemerenti qui vixit
annum et menses novem dies quinque
5 *qui cum soldu amatus fuisset*
a maiore
sua et vidit hunc morti constitutum
esse petivit de aeclesia ut fidelis de
seculo recessisset.[1]

Dedicated to the departed.
Florentius made this inscription
for his worthy son Apronianus who lived
one year and nine months and five days.
As he was truly loved by his grandmother
and she knew that his death was imminent,
she asked the church that he might
depart from the world as a believer.

We have here a case of private baptism in an emergency, which was administered to the one-and-three-quarter-year-old Apronianus in time and enabled him to die as a believer (*fidelis*). The very fact that it was the grandmother who urged that her darling should be baptized before his death, makes it in the highest degree probable that the father of the child, Florentius, was a pagan. This conjecture is confirmed by the formula in the first line, strikingly pagan for a Christian third-century catacomb inscription: *dis manibus sacrum*.[2] We have thus in the Apronianus inscription evidence before us for a missionary baptism administered to a twenty-one-month old dying non-Christian infant.

[1] *ILCV* I 1343; F. J. Dölger, *Ichthys* II 524, Rome, Catacomb of Priscilla.
[2] G. Greeven, *Die Siglen DM auf altchristlichen Grabschriften und ihre Bedeutung* (Diss. Erlangen, 1895), Rheydt, 1897. The Christian epitaphs which include the initials DM constitute 'an exceedingly small proportion' of all ancient Christian inscriptions (p. 150), and the majority of them belong to the fourth and fifth centuries (p. 158).

2

The Baptism of Children Born to Christian Parents in the Earliest Period

WHAT HAS BEEN said above about infant baptism on the admission of Jewish and Gentile parents to Christianity does not allow us to make any inference about the baptism of children born to Christian parents. Indeed, if we do not carefully distinguish these two questions we shall make it impossible for ourselves to get a clear historical view of the earliest times. While the first question was fairly easy to answer, the second is considerably more difficult.

I. THE NEW TESTAMENT

What did the primitive Church do when a child was born to Christian parents? Were these children immediately baptized? Or was the baptism delayed? Or was the baptism omitted in these cases? For that too would be conceivable. But this does not complete the list of questions which rise in the context. For particularly in relation to our problem we are not justified in presupposing without further ado a uniform practice in the primitive Church. We must rather reckon with the possibility that the practice was different in Jewish Christian circles from what it was in Gentile Christian circles, because here as there the practice was different in respect of circumcision. The Judaizers who demanded that the Gentile Christians should let themselves be circumcised,[1] unquestionably circumcised their own male children. Did they in addition have them baptized? Or were they content with circumcising them? Matters were different on Gentile Christian territory. In the fields of Paul's missionary activity children born of a Christian marriage were not circumcised. In the case of children of parents of Gentile birth we learn this from Gal.

[1] Gal. 5.2; Acts 15.1.

5.2; in the case of children of parents of Jewish birth it is asserted in Acts 21.21. Was baptism, the 'circumcision of Christ' (Col. 2.11), here a rite substituted for circumcision?

However many questions arise here, we must content ourselves with the small amount of information that we have. There are unfortunately only three passages which might give us some grounds for judging how the earliest age dealt with children born to Christian parents: I Cor. 7.14c, Acts 21.21, and Mark 10.13–16 and par. The first passage takes us on to Pauline territory, the second to Jewish Christian and Pauline territory, and the third to Rome.

(a) I Cor. 7.14c

We turn first to the difficult and disputed passage I Cor. 7.14c. Paul is speaking in I Cor. 7.12–16 of mixed marriages.[1] He ordains that the Christian member of a mixed marriage should not on his own initiative attempt to dissolve the marriage (7.12,13), and justifies this command with the words 'For the unbelieving husband is sanctified in the wife, and the unbelieving wife in the brother: else were your children unclean; but now are they holy' (7.14). The anxiety, says Paul, lest the non-Christian member of a mixed marriage defile the Christian member, is wholly unjustified, and therefore gives no ground for the dissolution of the marriage. Quite the reverse! The Christian member sanctifies—through the life of wedlock[2]—the non-Christian member. In proof thereof Paul refers to the children: 'Otherwise, your children would be unclean, but as it is they are holy.' Your children are indeed holy! This statement —of this Paul is certain—will be denied by no one in Corinth. No one can find it in his heart to say that the children of a mixed marriage are impure. Resting upon this Paul reassures the Christian partners in mixed marriages and says to them, 'If you concede that your children are holy, although their father (or mother) is an unbeliever, then you can continue your marriage without anxiety. Just as your children are sanctified by you so is your heathen husband or wife.' One believing member sanctifies the whole household; that is one of the most tremendous things that the

---

[1] On v. 16 cf. Jeremias, 'Die missionarische Aufgabe in der Mischehe (I Cor. 7.16)', in *Neutestamentliche Studien für Rudolf Bultmann*, pp. 255–60: since τίς οἶδεν εἰ or πόθεν οἶδας εἰ both in secular Greek and in Jewish Greek has the same sense 'perhaps', v. 16 is to be translated 'perhaps indeed you, the wife, can save your husband . . .'

[2] So most of the Fathers interpret (see below, pp. 45 f.); and emphatically J. Chr. K. von Hofmann, *Die heilige Schrift neuen Testaments* II 2. *Der erste Brief Pauli an die Korinther*[2], Nördlingen, 1874, pp. 142 f.; and in more recent times H. Lietzmann, *An die Korinther I, II* (Handbuch zum NT 9)[3], Tübingen, 1931, p. 31, which refers to I Cor. 6.15 f.

New Testament says about marriage. Since the apostle's argument from analogy from the holiness of the children to the sanctification of the heathen partner is only cogent if the children, like the heathen partner, are not baptized, we conclude that the holiness of the children rests *not on baptism, but on their descent from a Christian father or a Christian mother*.[1]

We can go one step further. Paul, as we have already seen, takes it for granted that the proposition, 'But now are your children holy', was generally acknowledged. He is indeed arguing *e concessis*, and bases his conclusion on this proposition. But where does the proposition come from? It is hard to believe that there was in Corinth a special doctrine about the holiness of children of mixed marriages. It is far more probable that the proposition, 'But now are your children holy', was held to be true of all children born in the Church. That would be the best explanation of the fact that Paul can without more ado assume that everyone in Corinth will agree that the proposition holds good of the children of a mixed marriage. If that is correct, then we must conclude that not only the children of a mixed marriage but all the children in the fellowship were counted holy, because they came of Christian parents.

The fact that Paul uses the word ἅγιος in I Cor. 7.14c without reference to baptism did not escape the theologians of the ancient Church and caused them great difficulty, and it does all honour to their love of the truth that the great majority of them did not flinch from facing the problem. The very first of them to give an exegesis on I Cor. 7.14c, Tertullian, traces the holiness of the children back to the *seminis praerogativa*,[2] as do Ephraem (died 373)[3] and the Ambrosiaster commentary (366/84).[4] In 393 Paulinus of Nola consults Jerome about the difficulty that I Cor. 7.14c speaks of a holiness not mediated by baptism, and Jerome does not deny it.[5] Chrysostom too (died 407),[6] Cyril of Alexandria

---

[1] This is today generally recognized. See the survey of the exegesis in G. Delling's 'Nun aber sind sie heilig', in *Gott und die Götter*, Festgabe für E. Fascher, Berlin, 1958, pp. 84–93, here pp. 84–87.

[2] *De Anima* 39.4. In addition he mentions the future Christian education (see below, p. 84).

[3] S. Ephraemi Syri *Commentarii in epistolas D. Pauli* etc., Venice, 1893, pp. 60 f.; quoted by Oepke, 'Urchristentum und Kindertaufe', *ZNW* 29, 1930, p. 84: *Quod si putaverit vir fidelis inquinatum iri matrimonium suum per infidelem consortem, sciat, quod sanctum est semen viri infidelis in utero mulieris fidelis; similiter et foetus mulieris infidelis sanctificatus est ratione viri fidelis. Sin autem id, quod dixi, ita non esset, ergo filii eorum iuxta mentes illorum immundi essent : nunc autem adhuc sancti sunt, si permanserint in fide, quam tradidi illis.*

[4] *Comm. on I Cor.* 7.14 (*MPL* 17, 219; Oepke, *ibid.*): *sancti sunt; quia de coniugiis licitis nati sunt.*

[5] *Ep.* 85. 2,5 (*CSEL* 55, pp. 136 f.).

[6] *Hom. in I Cor.* 19.3, on 7.14 (*MPG* 61, 155): εἰ γὰρ ἀκάθαρτος μένουσα γεννᾷς, τὸ δὲ παιδίον οὐκ ἀπό σου μόνης, ἀκάθαρτον ἄρα τὸ παιδίον, ἢ ἐξ ἡμισείας καθαρόν · νυνὶ δὲ οὐκ

(died 444)[1] and Theodoret (died *c*. 466)[2] support this exegesis, which the context itself demands.

What is the origin of this concept of holiness which deviates from the customary Pauline usage, which regards 'made holy' as a synonym of 'baptized'? The answer to this question can be discovered from the fact that the whole verse, I Cor. 7.14, 'For the unbelieving husband is consecrated (ἡγίασται) through his wife, and the unbelieving wife is consecrated through her husband. Otherwise, your children would be unclean (ἀκάθαρτα), but as it is they are holy', uses in fact the terminology of Jewish ritual. First of all this is obvious in the case of the expression ἀκάθαρτα, which is taken from the language of the Levitical purification ceremonies. The same is true also of the use of the verb ἁγιάζεσθαι in 7.14ab, which is quite without parallel in Paul, inasmuch as this sanctification' when used of Gentiles expresses an objective judgment valid independent of faith; that is Jewish and not Pauline usage.[3] And lastly the sentence 'Your children are holy', v. 14c, is also in the language of Jewish ritual, and it has its analogy in the law concerning proselytes. For Judaism disinguishes between children who were begotten and born 'not in holiness' (i.e. before conversion to Judaism), and children who were begotten and born 'in holiness' (i.e. after conversion to Judaism).[4] The former were baptized when the parents changed their religion, the latter were not. We know this because the question is raised what should be done in the borderline case where a pregnant Gentile woman changes her religion—i.e. where the begetting had been 'not in holiness' but the birth was 'in holiness'. The answer to this casuistical question is given by the sentence already quoted in another connection: 'If a non-Israelite woman becomes a proselyte during her pregnancy, her child does *not* need the baptismal bath.'[5] That means the birth is the decisive moment. Children who were born after their mother changed her religion do not have proselyte baptism administered to them. Their

---

ἐστιν ἀκάθαρτον. Cf. J. A. Cramer, *Catenae in S. Pauli Epp. ad Corinthios*, Oxford, 1841, p. 133; Oepke, 'Urchristentum und Kindertaufe,' *ZNW* 29, 1930, p. 84.

[1] Catena on I Cor. 7.12–14 (Cramer, p. 132; also cited by Oepke, *loc. cit.*): εὐλογοῦμεν μᾶλλον τοὺς οὔπω πιστεύσαντας, ἢ μολυνόμεθα παρ' αὐτῶν. « ἡγίασται γάρ,» φησίν, « ὁ ἀνὴρ ὁ ἄπιστος ἐν τῇ γυναικί.» οὕτως εἰσὶν ἅγια καὶ τὰ τέκνα ἡμῶν, νικῶντος πάντως που τοῦ ἐν τοῖς πιστεύουσιν ἁγιασμοῦ, τῶν οὔπω πεπιστευκότων τὸν ῥύπον.

[2] *Ad. loc.* (*MPG* 82, 277); Oepke, *loc. cit.*: ἔχει [ὁ ἀνὴρ ὁ ἄπιστος] σωτηρίας ἐλπίδα. Εἰ δὲ καὶ αὐτὸς . . . ἐπιμένοι τῇ νόσῳ [of unbelief], τὸ ἐκείνου σπέρμα μεθέξει τῆς σωτηρίας.

[3] Oepke, *op. cit.*, p. 85; H. Braun, 'Exegetische Randglossen zum I Korintherbrief', *Theologia Viatorum* 1, 1948/9, pp. 26–50; here pp. 39–42.

[4] Keth. 4.3; Yeb. 11.2; Tos. Bekh. 6.3 (540); Tos. Yeb. 12.2 (254); b. Sanh. 57b, 58a (Bar); b. Yeb. 42a, 98a.

[5] b. Yeb. 78a, see above, p. 39.

status is like that of Jewish children.[1] Anyone who was born 'in holiness' did not need the baptismal bath. This terminology of the law concerning proselytes is adopted in I Cor. 7.14c, when Paul says that the children of Christian parents are not 'unclean', but 'holy'. Here the rule holds, 'If the root is holy, so are the branches' (Rom. 11.16b).

What is the bearing of these facts upon the question whether in Corinth the children of Christian marriages were baptized? One would be tempted at first to draw the following conclusion: 'If in later Judaism children born "in holiness" were not baptized, then we must assume that the Christian Church also forbore to baptize the children of Christian parents. In this case, children born *before* their parents joined the Church would have been baptized, but not those born "in holiness".' This view was held and very precisely formulated by E. Ménégoz as long ago as 1884: 'To the question, "Did Paul baptize children?" we shall accordingly answer, "Yes and no. Yes, he baptized, along with their parents, the children of Gentiles who were converted to Christianity. No, he did not baptize the children born of Christian parents."[2]' I also argued in this way as recently as in the German edition of the present work.

I have, however, begun to doubt the validity of this reasoning. For it overlooks the important fact that in Judaism all boys, whether their birth was 'in holiness' or not, were circumcised on the eighth day. Since, as Col. 2.11 f. tells us, in the Christian Church baptism was the rite which replaced circumcision, we must conclude that the fact that the children mentioned in I Cor. 7.14c were 'holy' from their birth does not preclude the possibility that they were baptized. Even in the case of an unbelieving husband in a mixed marriage, the fact that he was made holy by his marriage to a Christian partner did not make it unnecessary

---

[1] Interesting evidence for this similarity of status is provided by a (hitherto not satisfactorily explained) inscription of the Roman Torlonia Catacomb, which A. M. Schneider dates early in the third century: Εἰρήνη τρεζπτὴ (sic!) προσήλυτος πατρὸς καὶ μητρὸς Εἰουδέα Ἰοδραηλίτης ἔζησεν ἤτ(η) (sic!) γ μ(ῆνας) ζ ἡμ(έ)ρ(αν) α. 'Irene, foster-child, a proselyte on the father's and on the mother's side, a Jewess, an Israelite, lived 3 years 7 months 1 day' (H. W. Beyer and H. Lietzmann, *Jüdische Denkmäler* I: *Die jüdische Katakombe der Villa Torlonia in Rom* [Studien zur spätantiken Kunstgeschichte 4] Berlin-Leipzig, 1930, inscription no. 44, p. 37, plate 18; *CII* I 19 f., no. 21). The first thing to say is that πατρὸς καὶ μητρός certainly is to be taken with the preceding word προσήλυτος (against Lietzmann). Then the noticeable heaping of epithet on epithet makes very good sense. The little child Irene was an adopted child, the dead parents were both Gentiles by birth, but had been converted to Judaism; and yet the little girl has a right to the honourable title 'Jewess, Israelite' (not proselyte), because she had been born after the conversion of her parents to Judaism (and thus 'in holiness'); cf. Keth 4.3: 'If her conception and birth (that of the daughter of a proselyte woman) was in holiness, then she counts in every respect as a daughter of Israel.'

[2] 'Le baptême des enfants d'après les principes de la théologie paulinienne', *Revue Chrétienne* 31, 1884, p. 242.

for him to be converted and baptized![1] *We must accordingly be content with the conclusion that I Cor. 7.14c bears no reference to baptism.* There is every probability that the statement, 'For your children are holy', no more excluded the baptism of children on the eighth day, in place of circumcision, than the saying, 'Your unbelieving husband is holy', excluded the later baptism of the husband. But here we cannot get beyond conjecture.

(b) Acts 21.21

The next passage which we must examine, in order to see whether it gives us any information about how the primitive Church dealt with children born in Christian marriage, is Acts 21.21. This passage takes us to Jerusalem. On his arrival there at Pentecost in the year 55 Paul is informed that grave suspicions have been roused in law-observing Jerusalem Jewish Christians, because it is reported that he forbids Jewish-Christian parents to have their children circumcised after their birth. 'They have been told about you that you teach all the Jews (Jewish Christians) who are among the Gentiles[2] to forsake Moses, telling them not to circumcise their children or observe the other customs.' From this passage we learn that in AD 55 new-born male infants of the Jerusalem Church were circumcised. Were they baptized in addition, as the Donatist Cresconius reports about 400 was the practice of the Symmachians: 'They are called Symmachians, and they have the circumcision of the Jews and the baptism of the Christians.' (*Symmachiani appellantur et circumcisionem habent Iudaeorum et baptismum christianorum*),[3] as is still customary today in the Coptic and the Abyssinian churches?[4]

At the same time, we learn from Acts 21.21 that in Pauline territory parents of Jewish (and all the more of heathen) descent did not have their male children circumcised on the eighth day after birth. Since Paul designates baptism as the ritual which replaces circumcision (Col. 2.11, see above, pp. 39 f.), *it is very probable that these children were baptized.*

(c) Mark 10.13–16

This conclusion is supported by the third passage listed above, *the*

---

[1] W. Metzger, 'Wird in I Kor. 7.14c ein Taufverzicht sichtbar?', *Deutsches Pfarrerblatt* 59, 1959, pp. 269–71.

[2] By the 'Jews' who, in the dispute about circumcision of children, obey Paul's instructions, naturally only Jewish Christians can be meant.

[3] Quoted in Augustine, *Contra Cresconium* I 31.36 (about 406); cf. Ambrosiaster, *Comm. on Gal.*, prologue (*MPL* 17, 337 f.). Cf. H. J. Schoeps, *Theologie und Geschichte des Judenchristentums*, Tübingen, 1949, p. 138.

[4] E. Nestle, *Philologia Sacra: Bemerkungen über die Urgestalt der Evangelien und Apostelgeschichte*, Berlin, 1896, p. 53.

pericope of the blessing of the children by Jesus (Mark 10.13–16, par. Matt. 19.13–15; Luke 18.15–17). The narrative itself, indeed, as we must emphasize, has nothing to do with baptism, but is 'pre-sacramental'.[1] It depicts an incident from the time of Jesus' ministry which—as we can say with fair certainty—must have happened on the evening of a Day of Atonement.[2] Parents[3] bring their children to Jesus 'that he may touch them' (Mark 10.13). What led the parents to make this request, and what its meaning was, is seen from Soph. 18.5:[4] 'It was a beautiful custom in Jerusalem to make the little children, boys and girls, fast on the fast-day (i.e. on the Day of Atonement), those who were a year old until daybreak, the twelve-year-olds till evening, and then to carry or lead them to the elders (i.e. the scribes) for them to bless them, strengthen (i.e. exhort) and pray for them, that they might one day attain to knowledge of the Torah and to good works.' Although the children did not need to fast on the Day of Atonement,[5] in pious families they were made to fast, even the smallest children (the latter at least until sunrise). And then they were brought to the scribes that they might pray for them (Matt. 19.13), and lay their hands on them in blessing (Mark 10.16). A group of parents came also to Jesus, and perhaps the rejection of the parents by the disciples can be explained as arising out of the situation described; the disciples reject the idea that Jesus should be treated as on a level with the scribes. Jesus' displeasure at the rejection was great (ἠγανάκτησεν: only in Mark 10.14 is this sharp word used of Jesus). The parents of the children understood his message better than the disciples! 'Let the children come to me, do not hinder them.' The promise that they are to have a share in God's coming Kingdom belongs also to children,[6] or rather, this promise is only[7] for such as are like children—children are small and can say 'Abba'[8] (Mark 10.14; it is uncertain whether v. 15 originally belongs to our story, since Matthew puts the verse in another place, viz. 18.3). So it is a word of repentance that Jesus speaks to his disciples in this story which occurred on the evening of the Day of

[1] H. Windisch, 'Zum Problem der Kindertaufe in Urchristentum', *ZNW* 28, 1929, p. 119.

[2] 10 Tishri (Sept.-Oct.).

[3] Notice the masculine in Mark 10.13b, which is interpreted by Luke 2.27, where an analogous masculine (αὐτούς) refers to 'the parents'.

[4] I quote from the Babylonian Talmud, Lemberg, 1861.

[5] Yoma 8.4.

[6] The ἐστίν of Mark 10.14b, without equivalent in Aramaic, has a future sense, as e.g. in Matt. 5.3, 10.

[7] The Semitic is inclined to omit the word 'only' where it is necessary in English Cf. J. Jeremias, *The Parables of Jesus*, ET 1954, p. 28 n. 35.

[8] See *op. cit.*, pp. 133 f.; T. W. Manson, *The Teaching of Jesus*[2], Cambridge 1935 p. 331.

D

Atonement (i.e. the Day of Repentance); only[1] to those whose whole life is a Day of Atonement, a becoming small before God, is entry under God's rule guaranteed. The story closes with the picture of the Lord taking the children in his arms and laying his hands upon them and blessing them.

Now every incident in the Synoptic Gospels has a twofold historical place; the one is the unique concrete situation in the life of Jesus, and the other the preaching and teaching of the primitive Church. Now we turn to the second *Sitz im Leben* of our story and ask 'Why did the primitive Church hand down the story? What in it was important for the Church?' A first answer arises out of the placing of our passage between the discussion about divorce (Mark 10.1–12) and the story of the rich young ruler (10.17–31). In this way there resulted a little catechism which instructed the churches how the disciples of Jesus should look on marriage, children, possessions. The middle section of this *didache*, which deals with the children (10.13–16), says accordingly to the Church, 'Hear how the Saviour calls the children, how he promises them a share in the eschatological salvation. To lead children to him is the task and responsibility of Christian parents.'

We must, however, define more precisely the significance which the passage about the blessing of the children possessed as guidance for Christian parents. Not only was the general summons to lead the children to Jesus by precept and example inferred from it, but also the command to give them to him through baptism. The very first place in which our passage appears in early Christian literature (Tertullian, *De Baptismo* 18.5)[2] shows that about 200, the words of Jesus, 'Let the children come to me, and do not forbid them' (Matt. 19.14), were generally understood as an injunction to let children be baptized, and even Tertullian, although in *De Baptismo* 18 he opposes a too early age for baptism, does not, as we shall see, try to escape from this interpretation of the passage as applying to baptism.[3] Similarly the *Apostolic Constitutions* base their claim that young children (νήπια) should be baptized on the words 'Forbid them not.'[4] The application of the passage about the blessing of the children to baptism was not first made at the end of the second century, but must be considerably older. There are several observations

---

[1] See p. 49 n. 7
[2] E. Massaux, *Influence de l'Évangile de saint Matthieu sur la littérature chrétienne avant saint Irénée*, Louvain-Gembloux, 1950. Herm., *Sim.* 9.29.3 (cf. 9.31.3) refers to Matt. 18.3, not to our *pericope*.
[3] See below, pp. 83 f.
[4] VI 15.7 (Funk, I 339).

we can make about the text which combine to suggest this conclusion.[1]

1. First we conclude with certainty from the Gospel of John that the verse Mark 10.15=Luke 18.17 was early interpreted as referring to baptism. This becomes clear if the five formulations in which this logion is handed down to us are laid synoptically before us.

Matt. 18.3	Mark 10.15 =Luke 18.17	John 3.5*	Justin, Apol. I 61.4	Const. Apost. VI 15.5
a. ᾿Αμὴν λέγω ὑμῖν	᾿Αμὴν λέγω ὑμῖν	᾿Αμὴν ἀμὴν λέγω σοι,		
b. ἐὰν μὴ	ὃς ἂν μὴ	ἐὰν μή τις	ἂν μὴ	ἐὰν μή τις
c. στραφῆτε κ. γένησθε	δέξηται τὴν β.τ.θ.	γεννηθῇ ἐξ ὕδατος καὶ πνεύματος (γεννηθῇ ἄνωθεν),	ἀναγεννηθῆτε,	βαπτισθῇ ἐξ ὕδατος καὶ πνεύματος,
ὡς τὰ παιδία	ὡς παιδίον,			
d. οὐ μὴ εἰσέλθητε	οὐ μὴ εἰσέλθῃ	οὐ δύναται εἰσελθεῖν (ἰδεῖν)	οὐ μὴ εἰσέλθητε	οὐ μὴ εἰσέλθῃ
εἰς τὴν β.τ. οὐρ.	εἰς αὐτήν.	εἰς (-) τὴν β.τ.θ.	εἰς τὴν β.τ. οὐρ.	εἰς τὴν β.τ. οὐρ.

* The variants from v. 3 are bracketed.

That in all five formulations we have to do with one and the same saying appears from the agreement in structure: (a) in all four Gospels the logion is introduced by 'Truly' (ἀμήν; John+ἀμήν) 'I say unto you' (λέγω ὑμῖν; John, 'thee', σοι); (b) in all the formulations a negative condition is added ('unless', ἐὰν μή; 'whoever does not', ὃς ἐὰν μή), (c) this condition deals in all the formulations (except in the Apostolic Constitutions) with becoming a child or being born again; (d) lastly, the apodosis has the same threatening sound in all formulations, with its 'not enter' (οὐ μὴ εἰσελθεῖν εἰς; John 3.3: 'see', ἰδεῖν) 'the kingdom

[1] See for the following, J. Jeremias, 'Mk. 10.13-16 Parr. und die Übung der Kindertaufe in der Urkirche', ZNW 40, 1941, pp. 243-45.

of God' (τὴν βασιλείαν τοῦ θεοῦ) or 'of heaven' (τῶν οὐρανῶν). The material, however, which is used to illustrate the condition for admission under the rule of God, is different (c). While the Synoptics (I–II) (among whom Matthew's version is most sharply coloured by Semitic turns of phrase)[1] speak of ' becoming-a-child-again' (Matthew) or 'receiving the kingdom of God like a little child' (Mark, Luke), John (III) speaks of ⁓ 'being-born-again'. The Synoptics thus lay more emphasis on the human attitude (ὡς παιδίον—'by becoming like a child'), and John on the action of God. In essence, however, both say the same: a complete new beginning of life is the precondition of anyone's finding admission under the rule of God. For our purposes it is important that the Gospel of John says clearly and unmistakably that the new beginning described by Jesus as indispensable is given *through baptism* ('of water and the Spirit', ἐξ ὕδατος καὶ πνεύματος). The fourth formulation of our saying (Justin, *Apol.* I 61.4) is commonly reckoned a quotation from John 3.5 (III), especially as Justin in the following sentence makes an allusion to John 3.4; accordingly our passage is regularly cited in introductory manuals to the New Testament as evidence that Justin used the Gospel of John, although there is nowhere in Justin a demonstrable word for word quotation from the Gospel of John. Even formulation IV is not in that category, but is instead a reproduction of Matt. 18.3, and is only influenced in the one word ἀναγεννηθῆτε by John 3.3 (γεννηθῇ ἄνωθεν). Since formulation IV recurs word for word (only enlarged by additions) in Clement of Alexandria (*Protrepticus* 9.82) and in the *Pseudo-Clementines* (*Homilies* 11.26.2 and *Recognitions* 6.9), it must certainly have had an independent circulation. Although Justin knew the Nicodemus story, he follows in his wording (formulation IV) the oral tradition.[2] This conclusion adds significance to the fact that Justin and the Pseudo-Clementine writings also, like John 3, bring our verse into relation to baptism, and quote it in the context of a description of baptism intended for non-Christians, and indeed, as an authority for the rite. Lastly, the formulation of the logion in *Apostolic Constitutions* (V), a free reproduction of John 3.5 showing synoptic influences in the apodosis, mentions baptism expressly ('unless

---

[1] στραφῆτε, Aram. *tubh*, 'become . . . again'; the way also in which ὡς combined with a substantive replaces an adjective is a Semitism (see Arndt and Gingrich, s.v. III. 3); τὰ παιδία: determined by the article in spite of indeterminate significance; τῶν οὐρανῶν: a periphrasis for the name of God.

[2] Cf. W. Bousset, *Die Evangeliencitate Justins des Märtyrers in ihrem Wert für die Evangelienkritik*, Göttingen, 1891, pp. 116–18; further E. Molland, 'La circoncision, le baptême, et l'autorité du décret apostolique (Actes XV 28 sq.) dans les milieux judéo-chrétiens des Pseudo-Clémentines,' *ST* 9, 1955, pp. 1–39, here p. 18 n. 1; H. Köster, 'Geschichte und Kultus im Johannesevangelium und bei Ignatius von Antiochien,' *ZTK* 54, 1957, pp. 56–69, here p. 63.

a man is baptized', ἐὰν μή τις βαπτισθῇ). We see then that, as early as the end of the first century AD, Mark 10.15 = Luke 18.17 was applied to baptism.

2. A further indication that when the passage about the blessing of the children was read to the Church it was reminded of baptism, is contained in the word 'to forbid, hinder, prevent' (κωλύειν, Mark 10.14; Matt. 19.14; Luke 18.16). This has been shown by O. Cullmann when he drew attention to the fact that in a series of baptismal texts (Acts 8.36; 10.47; 11.17; Matt. 3.14; Ebionite Gospel quoted by Epiphanius, *Haer.* 30.13.8) the word κωλύειν recurs so regularly as to suggest the conjecture that we have here to do with the use of a formula.[1] He concludes, 'As early as the first century, whenever someone who had come to faith was brought for baptism, inquiry was made whether any hindrance existed, that is, whether the candidate had really fulfilled the conditions demanded.'[2] This thesis of Cullmann's is strongly supported by two considerations. Firstly, we know that an analogous procedure was in use among the Jews. 'A (Gentile) who wishes to become a Jew may not be received without further question.' First the purity of his motives must be tested. If the result is unsatisfactory, 'he is sent forth and goes on his way'.[3] In view of the detailed correspondence between primitive Christian and Jewish baptismal ritual which we noted on pp. 29–37, there is every probability that the practice of the primitive Church followed the Jewish pattern also in this point, that before a man was admitted for baptism, there was an inquiry into his motives.[4] Secondly, it was a weakness of Cullmann's thesis that its basis was very narrow; the evidence was practically confined to the New Testament.[5] It is all the more significant that E. Molland has established the survival of the use of the κωλύειν formula in reference to baptism in the *Pseudo-Clementine Homilies:* 'What hinders my being baptized today?' (τί οὖν κωλύει σήμερόν με βαπτισθῆναι; 13.5.1) and 'Now, nothing hinders her being baptized' (οὐκοῦν οὐδὲν κωλύει αὐτὴν βαπτισθῆναι, 13.11.2).[6] Even later, in the Syriac version of the Irene legend, there is evidence for this use of the κωλύειν

---

[1] 'Les traces d'une vieille formule baptismale dans le Nouveau Testament', *RHPR* 17, 1937, pp. 424–34, and *Baptism in the New Testament*, pp. 71–80.

[2] *Op. cit.*, p. 75.

[3] Ger. 1.1 f.; more briefly b. Yeb. 47a (Bar.). Cf. Daube, *The New Testament and Rabbinic Judaism*, pp. 106–40 ('A Baptismal Catechism'), here pp. 113–19 ('The Test').

[4] See also pp. 82 f., below, on the sponsors who stood surety for the candidates for baptism.

[5] This narrow basis made possible doubts as to the correctness of Cullmann's thesis, which were expressed by A. W. Argyle, 'O. Cullmann's Theory concerning κωλύειν', *ExpT* 67, 1955/56, p. 17.

[6] Molland, *op. cit.*, p. 22.

formula. As Irene asks her parents, King Licinius and Queen Licinia, to let themselves be baptized, they answer, 'And what is there to hinder it, beloved daughter ?'[1] So if there is no doubt about the truth of Cull-mann's conjecture that κωλύειν was the *terminus technicus* for the refusal of baptism, then the question arises whether this conclusion has not consequences for our interpretation of κωλύειν in Mark 10.14 par. Cullmann answers this question in the affirmative, and concludes that in the period in which the Gospel tradition took shape the question of infant baptism was a live one, and that the passage about the blessing of the children was used as an argument against doubts about it: 'forbid them not'—there is no obstacle to it.[2]

3. The *pericope* closes in Mark (10.16) and Matthew (19.15) with Jesus laying his hands on the children. But laying on of hands belongs to the ritual of baptism; its mention must have been a further reminder of baptism to those who heard the story.[3]

4. It appears that a further proof that the passage about the blessing of the children was used in the context of baptism is offered by the Lucan version. It is to be noted that instead of παιδία (Mark 10.13; Matt. 19.13) Luke says τὰ βρέφη (Luke 18.15, with the article). This change was not motivated by the narrative itself, and should be explained as arising from the *Sitz im Leben* of the passage. The early Church already practised child baptism as infant baptism,[4] and with this in mind Luke will have inserted the expression τὰ βρέφη.[5]

To sum up, we may state that the formulation of the passage Mark 10.13–16 and par. in several places contains indirect references to baptism.

---

[1] A. S. Lewis, *Select Narratives of Holy Women from the Syro-Antiochene or Sinai Palimpsest* (Studia Sinaitica 9), London, 1900, p. q'b 2 (ET, Studia Sinaitica 10, p. 131).

[2] Cullmann, *op. cit.*, pp. 77 f.

[3] Cf. Alan Richardson, *An Introduction to the Theology of the New Testament*, London, 1958, p. 361.

[4] See p. 56.

[5] With all due caution the question may be raised in passing as to whether some further peculiarities of the Lucan text (18.15–17) are not to be explained as arising from the liturgical use of the passage, especially the remarkable omission of Mark 10.16 in Luke. The usual explanation, that Luke omitted the description of Jesus taking up the children in his arms and blessing them, because this emotion of Jesus was offensive to him, is extremely unsatisfactory, especially as Luke would in this way have deprived the passage of its conclusion. As can be seen from a study of the texts handed down to us dealing with the Last Supper, the liturgical use of texts brings into prominence elements that are universally valid to the detriment of what is historically unique. When we take this tendency into account we are led to give a different reason for the omission of the concluding passage here in Luke. We note further that the introduction of the words of Jesus in Luke (18.16) has been transformed in such a way that they appear no longer to be addressed to the disciples (as in Mark 10.14) but to the parents, who would be addressed if a liturgical use were made of the passage. Lastly, we must mention the prominent article τὰ βρέφη (Luke 18.15 over against παιδία, Mark 10.13; Matt. 19.13) which gives the passage a general character.

This suggests the conclusion that the narrative of the blessing of the children was important for the early Church not only on other grounds, but because the Church took it as authority for the practice of infant baptism.[1] We may conclude from this that in Rome at the time when the Gospel of Mark was written the children of Christian parents were baptized. In so doing, appeal was made to the example of Jesus, who had forbidden that children should be turned away from him, and had explicitly promised them a share in the coming kingdom of God (10.14).

2. SPECIAL EVIDENCE

For the first century we have no special evidence for the baptism of Christian children. In the second it was already taken for granted. We shall see how the unambiguous testimony of Origen, four times repeated, that it is the custom of the Church to baptize children in the very earliest days of their lives, is for two reasons especially important. First, it takes us a long way back from the time in which Origen writes (230–250) into the second century. And secondly, it holds good not only for Egypt and Palestine but also for almost the whole eastern Church (see p. 70). As for the West, the Western Text of Acts 2.39 allows us to make a cautious conjecture as to the baptism of Christian children before AD 150 (see p. 72). To this may be added a statement of Tertullian as evidence for Africa, leading us once more into the second century and expressly confirmed by evidence from literary sources and inscriptions dating from the time immediately following (see pp. 83–85). For all matters of detail we must refer the reader to Chapter 3. At this point we need only to emphasize that in fact the amount of evidence is much larger; we have confined ourselves to those instances which expressly state, or whose context informs us, that they refer to the children of Christian parents. An exact description of the parents is however very often missing. It is typical that among the many third-century epitaphs of children dating from about AD 200 onwards and discussed below (pp. 75–80, 85 f.), only two give definite information about the religious status of the parents. One is that of Zosimus who died at the age of two, who is described as πιστὸς ἐκ πιστῶν and thereby as the baptized child of Christian parents, since, according to established usage, the word πιστός describes a baptized person (as contrasted with a catechumen).[2]

---

[1] Cf. J. Leipoldt, 'Die altchristliche Taufe religionsgeschichtlich betrachtet,' *WZU Leipzig* 3, 1953/4, p. 67a, n. 1: 'The narrator must have been thinking of infant baptism.'
[2] Dölger, *Ichthys* V 729. Compare the Apronianus inscription (see above, pp. 41 f.: *fidelis*=baptized); Origen, *Comm. on Matt.* XV 36 (see below, pp. 65 f. n. 5).

Πιστὸς ἐκ πισ
τῶν Ζώσιμος
ἐνθάδε κεῖμε
ζήσας ἔτεσιν
β' μη(νὶ) α' ἡμέ(ραις) κε'[1]

I, Zosimus, a believer from
believers, lie here having
lived 2 years, 1 month, 25
days.

Tombstone inscription of the child Zosimus

The other inscription which gives information about the religious status of the parents is the following metrical Greek inscription of three boys of twelve years old, who are described as πιστοὶ γενετῇ; it comes perhaps also from the third century:[2]

> 'Αλκινόων δύο σῆμα 'Αλεξάνδρου τε συνέμων
> τρεῖς ⟨δὴ⟩ δωδεχέτεις πιστοὺς γενετῇ προέπενψα
>   ιχθυς
>   γ[3]

The phrase πιστοὶ γενετῇ is parallel to the πιστὸς ἐκ πιστῶν of the Zosimus inscription and implies that this is a case of baptized children of Christian parents. The parallel to the Zosimus inscription makes it probable that in the case of the three boys also baptism was administered at the earliest age.

We see then that East and West agree in their evidence for the baptism of Christian children for the second century. In so far as we have information about the age at which baptism was administered, the sources agree in saying that Christian children were baptized as babies (*parvuli*, *infantes*, νήπιοι, παιδία)[4] and, indeed, in the first days of their life.[5] Clearly the custom of circumcision was imitated on this point. *Delay of baptism in the case of Christian children was wholly unknown in the primitive Church.* It is not until the year 329–30 that we have certain evidence of a case of Christian parents letting their children grow up unbaptized.[6]

---

[1] Dölger, *Ichthys* I[2] 201; V 728 f., Plates 171.1 and 19.61; Kraft 36. Place of origin unknown, now in the Lateran Museum. A. M. Schneider dates the inscription to the later third century.

[2] Dölger, *op. cit.*, I[2] 200.

[3] Dölger, *op. cit.*, 199–203; CIG IV 551, no. 9715; Kraft 36, Rome.

[1] Origen, see pp. 65 f.; Cyprian, p. 85; inscriptions, pp. 55 f., 75–80, 85; cf. Irenaeus, pp. 72 f.

[5] Origen, Cyprian, inscriptions, see previous note.   [6] See below, p. 89.

3. FURTHER CONFIRMATION OF THIS VIEW

Our conclusion, that in the Gentile Church (we have no information about the Jewish Christian Church) children born in the fellowship were baptized as early as the first century, receives confirmation from different sides.

1. We hear in the history of the early Church nothing about two kinds of Christians, baptized and unbaptized;[1] had baptism been withheld from children born to Christian parents, then there would very soon have grown up a mixed crowd of baptized and unbaptized Christians living alongside of each other.[2]

2. We have no information about the introduction of a practice deviating from previous custom. In particular, nowhere in the literature of the ancient Church do we find discussions on the question whether children of Christian parents should be baptized. Had the custom of baptizing them not been introduced until the second century, it would have been quite inconceivable that the introduction of so startling a novelty would have left no trace in the sources, which begin to be more abundant at this time.

3. The fact that no special rite for child baptism was introduced speaks also for the early practice of baptizing Christian children. Had the practice not been introduced until a time when the baptismal ritual had reached a rather fuller state of development, the Church would surely not have been content simply to apply the ritual of adult baptism to children.

4. Nowhere does the custom appear as the special doctrine of a party or sect. What we have before us is rather one of the few Church usages in relation to which the great Church everywhere was completely unanimous.[3] Even Tertullian shares this unanimity; however lively, at least on occasion, may have been his plea for the postponement of the baptism of the children of pagans joining the Church, he took the baptism of Christian children for granted.[4]

5. To conclude, both East and West are at one in tracing infant

---

[1] A. Oepke, 'Zur Frage nach dem Ursprung der Kindertaufe', *L. Ihmels-Festschrift*, Leipzig, 1928, p. 100.

[2] Not until the Marcionite church do we find baptized and unbaptized persons together, but this is for quite different reasons (see pp. 69 f. below).

[3] Ph.-H. Menoud, 'Le baptême des enfants dans l'Église ancienne', *Verbum Caro* 2, 1948, p. 17.

[4] See below, pp. 83-85.

baptism back to apostolic tradition,[1] and it is highly questionable whether this tradition should be so quickly put on one side as a dogmatic *petitio principii*, as occasionally happens.[2] For the Gospel of John could scarcely have formulated in so unqualified a manner the proposition that only those begotten by water and the spirit can enter the kingdom of God (John 3.5), if in its time baptism had been withheld from children of Christian parents.

[1] West: Hippolytus, see below, pp. 73 f.; East: Origen, see below, p. 66.
[2] Cf. B. F. Kattenbusch, 'Taufe, II: Kirchenlehre,' *Realencyklopädie für protestantische Theologie und Kirche XIX*[3], Leipzig, 1907, pp. 403–24, here p. 408.

3

The Development up to the End of the Third Century[1]

HAVING DEALT in Chapters 1 and 2 with the origins of baptism in New Testament times, we turn now to the developments in the succeeding times up to the crisis which began in the fourth century. We begin with the East, for which the evidence is more scanty, and then pass on to the West, which provides more material.

1. THE EAST

A. *Asia Minor*

The first pieces of information from outside the New Testament which allow us to make an inference as to the practice of infant baptism are provided by Asia Minor. They are indeed of an indirect nature but they confirm each other. The oldest of them takes us back to apostolic times, probably to the years when the Gospels of Matthew and Luke were written.

In the old account of the martyrdom of Polycarp of Smyrna[2] given by

---

[1] W. Wall's scholarly collection of source-material, *The History of Infant Baptism*, 2 vols. London, 1674, can still be consulted with profit. (I used the two-volume edition, London, 1705). From more modern times one must cite H. Windisch, 'Zum Problem der Kindertaufe im Urchristentum', *ZNW* 28, 1929, pp. 134–42, and Ph.-H. Menoud's careful discussion of the patristic evidence, 'Le baptême des enfants dans l'Église ancienne', *Verbum Caro* 2, 1948, pp. 15–26, and J.-C. Didier, 'Un cas typique de développement du dogme. A propos du baptême des enfants', *MelScR* 9, 1952, pp. 191–214 (Literature). We owe to H. Kraft, *Texte zur Geschichte der Taufe, besonders der Kindertaufe in der alten Kirche* (Kleine Texte 174), Berlin, 1953 (henceforward quoted as 'Kraft'), a comparative survey of the most important passages in the original sources.

[2] According to *Mart. Polyc.* 18.3 the account was composed in the year of the martyrdom, but it is not certain that this verse is genuine; cf. H. von Campenhausen, *Bearbeitungen und Interpolationen des Polykarpmartyriums* (Sitzungsberichte der Heidelberger Akademie der Wissenschaften, phil.-hist. Klasse, 1957, 3), pp. 29 f.

the church in Smyrna, we are told that the grey-haired bishop when challenged to revile Christ, answered: 'For eighty-six years I have served him, and he never did me any wrong. How can I blaspheme my King who saved me?' (ὀγδοήκοντα καὶ ἓξ ἔτη δουλεύω αὐτῷ, καὶ οὐδέν με ἠδίκησεν· καὶ πῶς δύναμαι βλασφημῆσαι τὸν βασιλέα μου τὸν σώσαντά με;).[1] Before we investigate this sentence with reference to our theme, we must try to date it.

Here we must do some digging. There are two sources available to help us in dating the year of Polycarp's death:[2] (1) In his *Ecclesiastical History* Eusebius says that Polycarp suffered martyrdom under Marcus Aurelius[3] (161–180), and indeed—since Eusebius begins his long account of the events during the reign of Marcus Aurelius[4] with the martyrdom of Polycarp—in the early years of this emperor; more exactly, in a note in his *Chronicle* dealing with the seventh year of Marcus Aurelius' reign (167–68), he says that at that time Polycarp and the martyrs of Gaul (of Lyons) (!) fell victims to the persecution.[5] (2) *The Martyrdom of Polycarp* tells us in a chronological supplement that Polycarp μηνὸς Ξανθικοῦ δευτέρᾳ ἱσταμένου (on the second day at the beginning of the month Xanthikos), πρὸ ἑπτὰ καλανδῶν Μαρτίων (23 February), σαββάτῳ μεγάλῳ, ὥρᾳ ὀγδόῃ (on a great sabbath, at the eighth hour [i.e. 2 p.m.]), was put to death in the Proconsulate of Statius Quadratus,[6] i.e. on Saturday, 23 February 155, 166, 172 or 177, or on Saturday, 22 February 156 (leap year). Older authorities followed Eusebius and ascribed the martyrdom to Marcus Aurelius' reign (161–80), but in 1867 a change of opinion was caused by an investigation by W. H. Waddington.[7] Waddington identified a certain L. Statius Quadratus, who was recorded as Consul on an inscription in Ostia, with the Proconsul Statius Quadratus mentioned in the supplement to *Mart. Polyc.* 21, and on these grounds suggested the date 23 February 155, a suggestion which found almost universal acceptance.

Only a slight modification of this view was implied by the suggestion of E. Schwartz, who identified the 'Great Sabbath' of *Mart. Polyc.* 21

---

[1] 9.3. Reported in exactly identical form by Eusebius, *Hist. Eccl.* IV 15.20. This is important because his text of *Mart. Polyc.*, which unfortunately occasionally paraphrases and abbreviates the original, stands nearer to it than does the text of Pseudo-Pionius, which the editions follow. Cf. H. von Campenhausen, *op. cit.*, pp. 7–16.

[1] A good survey of the debate is given by J. A. Fischer, *Die Apostolischen Väter* (Schriften des Urchristentums I), Darmstadt, 1956, pp. 230–33.

[3] IV 15.1.   [4] IV 14.10–V 8.   [5] *GCS* 20 (Eusebius V), p. 222.

[6] *Mart. Polyc.* 21.

[7] 'Mémoire sur la Chronologie de la vie du rhéteur Aelius Aristide', *Mémoires de l'Institut Impérial de France: Academie des Inscriptions et Belles-Lettres* 26.1, Paris, 1867, pp. 203–68.

with the Sabbath before Passover, and put in a plea for the 22 February 156, a date very near the full moon.[1] It was not till 1951 that the debate was reopened by an essay of H. Grégoire and P. Orgels.[2] They declared that *Mart. Polyc.* 21 was a forgery and ascribed a *lapsus calami* to the text of Eusebius' *Chronicle* ('par suite d'une faute de copiste' the note about Polycarp and the martyrs of Gaul was put in the seventh year of Marcus Aurelius instead of the seventeenth),[3] and postponed the martyrdom of Polycarp to 23 February 177, which was the year of the martyrdoms in Lyons, which Eusebius indeed mentions in his *Chronicle* along with that of Polycarp. Though this daring hypothesis was rightly and almost universally opposed,[4] yet H. Grégoire and P. Orgels did a great service by their investigation, which challenged scholars to reopen the question of the date 155 or 156 which had been quite taken for granted.

Let us test the three days under discussion (23 February 155 or 22 February 156; after 161, to be more exact 167–8; and 23 February 177). We may at once, with the majority of scholars, exclude the year 177.

(*a*) This date is not only insufficiently supported by the sources (for the assumption of a slip of the pen can hardly count as textual support), but it also contradicts both Eusebius' dating of the martyrdom in the early years of Marcus Aurelius and what Irenaeus tells us.[5] All this is scarcely compatible with the year 177 as the date of Polycarp's death. Furthermore, this date is excluded by the fact that Irenaeus, who writes soon after 180, speaks of Polycarp's successors in the plural.[6]

---

[1] *Christliche und jüdische Ostertafeln* (Abhandlungen der Gesellschaft der Wissenschaften zu Göttingen, phil.-hist. Klasse N. F. 8.6), Berlin, 1905, pp. 127–31; 'Osterbetrachtungen', *ZNW* 7, 1906, pp. 1–33, here p. 9.

[2] 'La véritable date du martyre de S. Polycarp (23 février 177) et le "*Corpus polycarpianum*",' *Analecta Bollandiana* 69, 1951, pp. 1–38.

[3] *Op. cit.*, p. 23, cf. 27.

[4] E. Griffe, 'A propos de la date du martyre de Saint Polycarpe', *Bulletin de Littérature Ecclésiastique* (Toulouse), 52, 1951, pp. 170–77; 'Un nouvel article sur la date du martyre de saint Polycarpe', *op. cit.*, 54, 1953, pp. 178–81; P. Meinhold, 'Polykarpos (1)', Pauly-Wissowa, *Realencyclopädie XXI*, Stuttgart-Waldsee, 1952, cols. 1662–93, here cols. 1673–80; W. Telfer, 'The Date of the Martyrdom of Polycarp', *JTS*, n.s.3, 1952, pp. 79–83; H.-I. Marrou, 'La date du martyre de S. Polycarpe', *Analecta Bollandiana* 71, 1953, pp. 5–20. See also J. A. Fischer, *op. cit.*, p. 232.

[5] Irenaeus says, *Adv. Haer.* III 3.4 (quoted also by Eusebius, *Hist. Eccl.* IV 14.3), that Polycarp had been made a disciple by apostles, had held converse with many eyewitnesses of the Lord, and had been consecrated Bishop of Smyrna by apostles. Even if we need not weigh every word of Irenaeus, we can still infer from these utterances that the youth of Polycarp fell within the first century. This conclusion is supported also by the circumstance that already in the time of Ignatius (who suffered martyrdom under Trajan [98–117]) Polycarp was Bishop of Smyrna and was held in high esteem, without Ignatius emphasizing his youth as he did that of Bishop Damas of Magnesia (*Magn.* 3.1). In view of all this, Polycarp's birth cannot be dated so late as (177–86=) AD 91.

[6] *Adv. Haer.* III 3.4; in Eusebius, *Hist. Eccl.* IV 14.5.

(*b*) But 23 February 155 and 22 February 156 are also eliminated, quite apart from the questionable character of the textual evidence for them (*Mart. Polyc.* 21),[1] when we consider the journey of Polycarp to Bishop Anicetus at Rome, a journey for which Irenaeus is a reliable witness.[2] This journey would have to have occurred at the latest in the autumn preceding the martyrdom, before the end of the sailing season,[3] i.e. in autumn 154 or 155. But at that time, according to Eusebius, Anicetus had not yet even taken office, as Eusebius dates Anicetus' period of office from 157–68/9.[4] But even if, doubting the accuracy of Eusebius' chronology of the Roman bishops of the second century,[5] we are willing to date Anicetus' assumption of office several years earlier, we have still not escaped the difficulties which stand in the way of dating the martyrdom in 155 or 156. For at the time of his death, as the quotation given above from *Mart. Polyc.* 9.3 reliably informs us, Polycarp was at least eighty-six years old. But it is extremely improbable that so shortly before his death at so great an age he could have undertaken the journey from Smyrna to Rome and back, which even by ship was at that time an infinitely strenuous one.

(*c*) So only the date that Eusebius gives is left: Polycarp's martyrdom took place at the beginning of Marcus Aurelius' reign (161–80), to be more precise, in the year 167–8.[6]

Reckoning from this date we arrive at fairly reliable figures for Polycarp's life: birth about AD 80, journey to Rome[7] in the later seventies of his life, martyrdom barely ten years later.

If A. Oepke,[8] who here follows older authors, is right, as is most probably the case, the statement that Polycarp was eighty-six years old allows us to make an inference about the bishop's baptism. Consequently

---

[1] Called in question most recently by H. von Campenhausen: Chapter 21 'certainly cannot belong to the original' (*op. cit.*, p. 31).

[2] *Adv. Haer.* III 3.3 f.; Letter of Irenaeus to Bishop Victor of Rome (excerpt preserved in Eusebius, *Hist. Eccl.* V 24. 11–18; here 16 f.).

[3] *Mare clausum*: 11 November–5 March.

[4] *Hist. Eccl.* IV 19. The traditional dating of the years of office of Anicetus (155–166) given in the manuals and lexicons is wholly valueless. It has obviously been arrived at by accepting Eusebius' statement (*loc. cit.*) that Anicetus was eleven years in office, and yet dating his year of accession two years earlier to fit in with the theory that Polycarp was martyred on 22 February 156.

[5] H. Boehmer, 'Zur altrömischen Bischofsliste', *ZNW* 7, 1906, pp. 333–39; E. Caspar, *Die älteste römische Bischofsliste* (Schriften der Königsberger Gelehrten Gesellschaft, Geisteswiss. Klasse II 4), Berlin, 1926.

[6] W. Telfer, *op. cit.*, p. 83: A.D. 168; H.-A. Marrou, *op. cit.*: before 168/69; J. Vogt, 'Christenverfolgung I (historisch)', *RAC* II, 1954, cols. 1159–1208, here col. 1175: 167; H. von Campenhausen, *op. cit.*, pp. 5 f.: between 161 and 168/9, more probably towards the end of this period.

[7] This occurs, according to Eusebius, between 157 and 161; see below, p. 63 n. 1.

[8] 'Zur Frage nach dem Ursprung der Kindertaufe', *L. Ihmels-Festschrift*, pp. 54 f.

if Polycarp was martyred in 167-8 he must have been baptized in the year 81 or 82 in very early childhood. Now the question might indeed be asked if the date of his becoming a Christian eighty-six years earlier necessarily occurred in his very early childhood. Could Polycarp not have been converted in his youth, let us say—as some have conjectured— at fourteen years of age? But that leads us to impossibilities! In that case not only must Polycarp at the time of his martyrdom—however one may date the latter—have been a hundred years old (this is at least conceivable, though if it were the case it is hard to believe that this unusual fact would have been passed over in silence by the *Martyrium Polycarpi*), but worse still, he must have undertaken his journey to Bishop Anicetus at Rome, which according to Eusebius took place between 157 and 161,[1] between the age of ninety and ninety-four (if the martyrdom be dated in 155-6 at the great age of a hundred; if it be dated as late as 177 between the age of eighty and eighty-four), which is quite unthinkable. However one dates the martyrdom, the conclusion is inevitable that the eighty-six years for which Polycarp had served Christ up to the time of his death more or less cover his whole life. But then his parents must have been Christians (or at least must have become Christians very soon after his birth). Thus we have most probably in *Mart. Polyc.* 9.3 an indirect confirmation given us of the practice of infant baptism in the years round about AD 80.

In the case of Polycrates also, the Bishop of Ephesus, we have almost certainly a son of Christian parents, since in his message sent to Rome in 190-1 and dealing with the Easter Controversy he mentions that seven of his kinsmen were bishops and he himself was the eighth.[2] When he continues 'I now, my brethren, have lived in the Lord (ἔχων ἐν κυρίῳ) sixty-five years',[3] we may conclude that he was baptized as a child about AD 125.

Then Pliny's letter[4] written in 112/13 allows us to make an inference when it speaks of the very young (*teneri*) who along with the adults (*robustiores*) belong to the Church, and also of the many of all ages (*multi omnis aetatis*) who have been ensnared by the new faith. When we remember what Pliny says about the astonishingly quick spread of the

---

[1] *Hist. Eccl.* IV 14.1: still in the reign of Antoninus Pius (138-161); IV 14.19: consecration of Anicetus 157.

[2] Eusebius, *Hist. Eccl.* V 24.6.

[3] V 24.7.

[4] X 96.2: *nec mediocriter haesitavi, sitne aliquod discrimen aetatum, an quamlibet teneri nihil a robustioribus differant;* 96.9: *multi enim omnis aetatis, omnis ordinis, utriusque sexus etiam, vocantur in periculum et vocabuntur.* I have to thank my colleague Ernst Schaefer for this reference.

Christian faith in Bithynia, we may conclude with certainty that among the very young there were numerous children of parents who had been converts from heathenism; and since Pliny considers the possibility that the very young should be brought to trial and punished in the same manner as the adults, we must take it that they had become through baptism full members of the Church.

The *Acts of the Martyrs* supply further indirect evidence. According to the records of the trial of Carpus, Papylus and Agathonica (put to death probably under Marcus Aurelius, 161–80), which are acknowledged to be genuine, Papylus of Thyatira stated during the trial, 'I have served God from my youth up, and I have never sacrificed to idols, but am a Christian' (34). According to the equally trustworthy *Acts of Justin and his Companions* (put to death about 165 in Rome), similar statements were made by Euelpistus,[1] who came from Cappadocia, and Hierax,[2] whose home was in Iconium (Phrygia). And such testimonies are repeated in reports about martyrs of the third century in Asia Minor, to which certain legendary embellishments have been added.[3]

In concluding our discussion on Asia Minor, we must mention that the witness of Irenaeus (see pp. 72 f.) includes western Asia Minor, where he spent his youth and was a pupil of Polycarp of Smyrna, and that as we shall see, the witness of Origen in a similar manner includes eastern Asia Minor (see p. 70). Thus our evidence (which we frankly confess is only indirect) covers the whole of Asia Minor: the western part of it (the province of Asia), the north (Bithynia), the east (Cappadocia) and the south (Lycia and Pamphylia).

B. *Egypt*

Here we are on firmer ground. We shall indeed do well to disregard Clement of Alexandria. For when soon after 195 he speaks, in an allegorical figure, of the 'children who are drawn from the water' (by the fisher) (τῶν ἐξ ὕδατος ἀνασπωμένων παιδίων)[4] it is indeed possible that he is thinking of child baptism, but he might be thinking of children

---

[1] 4.7: 'I also received Christianity from my parents.'

[2] 4.5: 'I always have been, and shall ever be, a Christian.' Hierax' companion Paion, of whose home we are not told, says in 4.6, 'We received from our parents this good confession.'

[3] Maximus of Asia (put to death under Decius, 249/51) says in 1.10, 'I do not offer sacrifice except to the one God, to whom, I am glad to say, I have offered sacrifice from my earliest youth.' Conon of Magydus in Pamphylia (also put to death under Decius, 249/51?) says in 4.2 (p. 65), 'I have a family connection with Christ (συγγένεια πρὸς Χριστόν), whom I serve as did my forefathers.' Asterius of Lycia, in the *Acts of Claudius, Asterius and their Companions* (put to death probably in the third century), says in 2.2 (p. 107), 'I was taught by my parents to worship and love him (sc. the one God).'

[4] *Paedagogus* III 59.2.

Scale 1:6 cm

Clay coffin of a mummy of a child
Brit. Mus. 54051

in the faith (cf. I Peter 2.1 f.) whom the missionary brings to baptism.

Origen's witness, on the other hand, is of the greatest importance. Thrice he mentions that the baptism of infants (παιδία/parvuli) is a custom of the Church: in his *Homilies on Luke* (XIV on 2.22a: 'therefore children also are baptized', διὰ τοῦτο καὶ τὰ παιδία βαπτίζεται),[1] *Homilies on Leviticus* (VIII 3 on 12.2: baptism is given 'according to the custom of the Church, to infants also', *secundum ecclesiae observantiam etiam parvulis*),[2] and in his *Commentary on Romans* (V 9 on 6.5–7: 'For this reason, moreover, the Church received from the apostles the tradition of baptizing infants too', *pro hoc et ecclesia ab apostolis traditionem suscepit, etiam parvulis baptismum dare*). In all three places Job 14.4 f. (LXX) appears among the scriptural proofs adduced by Origen: 'No one is pure from stain, yea though he be but one day old.' From the stereotyped citation of this passage we conclude that when Origen speaks of παιδία or *parvuli* who are baptized, he means infants.

To these three passages we may add perhaps a fourth reference from the *Homilies on Joshua* IX 4,[3] which were written in 249–51. In his exegesis of Josh. 8.32 ('and he [Joshua] wrote there upon the stones a copy of the law of Moses, which he wrote in the presence of the children of Israel'), Origen asks how it was possible that Joshua had written the whole long book 'in the presence of the children of Israel' (*coram filiis Istrahel*): had not the people gone away in the interval? His answer is: Joshua's writing typifies the writing of the law in the heart of the man who turns to the Lord, and the *filii Istrahel* are not the people of Israel but the angels, who were present then as they are present at the baptism of every Christian. 'For if we are right in saying that "Israel" means him who sees God in the spirit, then that is even more true of the ministering angels—according to the saying of the Lord, who says of *infantes* (because thou wast also an *infans* at thy baptism [*quod et tu fuisti infans in baptismo*]) that "their angels always behold the face of my Father who is in heaven" (Matt. 18.10). So "in the presence of" these "children of Israel" who were present on that occasion when the *fidei sacramenta* were given to you "who see the face of God", Jesus[4] "wrote the copy of the law" in your heart.'[5]

---

[1] τὰ παιδία βαπτίζεται « εἰς ἄφεσιν ἁμαρτημάτων ». Ποίων ; Πότε γὰρ ἥμαρτον ; 'Αλλὰ μήποτε, ἐπεὶ « οὐδεὶς καθαρὸς ἀπὸ ῥύπου », τὸν ῥύπον δὲ ἀποτίθεταί τις διὰ τοῦ μυστηρίου τοῦ βαπτίσματος, διὰ τοῦτο καὶ τὰ παιδία βαπτίζεται.

[2] '*Nemo mundus a sorde, nec si unius diei sit vita eius.*' *Addi his etiam illud potest, ut requiratur, quid causae sit, cum baptisma ecclesiae pro remissione peccatorum detur, secundum ecclesiae observantiam etiam parvulis baptismum dari.*

[3] I owe this suggestion to my assistant, Christoph Burchard.

[4] Jesus and Joshua are seen as one, since their names are identical in Greek and Latin.

[5] There is an element of uncertainty in this proof, because *infans* could also be meant in a metaphorical sense. Infant baptism, though not expressly mentioned, is pre-

E

The passages quoted were written between 233 and 251,[1] but they take us back to a considerably earlier period. For Origen maintains—as Hippolytus, shortly before and independently of him, had done in Rome[2] —that infant baptism was a custom reaching back to apostolic times; *Ecclesia ab apostolis traditionem suscepit.*[3] He could hardly have expressed himself thus if he had not himself been baptized as a παιδίον/*parvulus*. (Origen was born in 185 in Egypt, probably in Alexandria; he was seventeen years old when his father was martyred in 202.) When we note that his family, as Eusebius credibly[4] informs us, had been Christian[5] for several generations (ἐκ προγόνων; Rufinus translates *ab avis atque atavis*), we must add that he could hardly have spoken of a 'tradition handed down from the apostles' had he not known that at least his father and probably also his grandfather had been baptized as παιδία. This means that the tradition of his family carries us back from the date of his own baptism at least to the date of his father's—i.e. to the middle of the second century, and probably even to the baptism of his grandfather in the first half of that century.

The mummy of an Egyptian child, which I noticed while visiting the British Museum in London, comes from approximately the time of Origen (No. 54051, Wallcase 42; see plate facing p. 64).[6] The attached inscription reads, 'Pottery coffin containing the mummy of a child. The symbol of the cross in the right hand suggests Christian parentage. Late Roman period, about AD 200.'[7] The clay coffin in the illustration measures 87 centimetres by 28, the mummy itself including its covering is only 74 centimetres long.[8] The coffin portrays a little girl with her hair dressed

---

supposed in another allegorical interpretation with which Origen concludes the exegesis in his *Commentary on Matthew* (after 244) of the parable of the workers in the vineyard (Matt. 20.1–16). In XV 36 the workers who were hired early in the morning are likened to 'those who are called from childhood and the earliest age of life (τοὺς μὲν ἐκ παίδων καὶ πρώτης ἡλικίας κληθέντας), who shortly afterwards are called οἱ ἐκ παίδων πιστοί (on πιστοί cf. p. 55).

[1] The *Homilies on Luke* after 233, the *Homilies on Leviticus* and the *Commentary on Romans* after 244, the *Homilies on Joshua* 249/51.

[2] See below, p. 74.

[3] See above, p. 65.

[4] Since Eusebius is opposing a contradictory statement by the anti-Christian writer Porphyry, he is bound to pay attention to accuracy.

[5] *Hist. Eccl.* VI 19.10. Rufinus, *ibid.*

[6] I have to thank Dr S. Morenz for his friendly advice and for the assurance that he agrees with the position outlined below.

[7] My colleague Dr J. Spiegel informs me, with reference to this date, that he would like to leave the whole of the third century open.

[8] By information kindly supplied by the British Museum, Department of Egyptian Antiquities (Mr I. E. S. Edwards), on 16 May 1957.

in ringlets; under the chin the beard of Osiris can be seen. The hands are crossed over the breast. In her left hand the child holds a lotus flower, the sign of rebirth; in her right hand—this is the astonishing thing—a cross with serrated ends and a long handle which ends in a ring, which itself constitutes the end of a chain which is twice wound round the body. I made inquiries of numerous colleagues in the field of Egyptology, who placed their knowledge most readily at my disposal,[1] and the conclusion was to the effect that there are no known analogies to our mummy, and a personal investigation in the Coptic Museum in Cairo confirmed this result.

The first point to clear up was whether the cross was to be considered as a Christian symbol and then (on account of the chain) as an amulet or whether it might be a heathen sign. The Egyptologists of whom I made inquiry were united and decisive in their rejection of the second possibility. At the most, they said, in view of the serrations at the ends of the transverse bar of the cross, and considering the fact that heathen mummies in many cases hold the symbol of life in their right hands, one might speak of a 'Christianized ankh-sign'.[2]

The next thing was to ask the age of the child enclosed in the mummy. This, I was informed, could not be exactly ascertained by its size, since there were different embalming procedures. In order to get a reliable answer we would have to examine the mummy by X-rays and make an estimate based on the condition of the teeth and bones. Thus the estimates varied between eighteen months and ten years. Perhaps I may mention as a clue that I saw in the Egyptian Museum in Cairo a mummy about 80 centimetres long (No. 33214, room 14) whose age, judging from the portrait upon it, I would estimate at four years. Since our mummy is smaller the child would be rather younger.

It is certain that we have here an example of Egyptian syncretism of the third century AD. Nor did those responsible break with the old custom of making the little girl Osiris by depicting his attributes on the coffin.[3] But the cross which was attached to the chain and hung round her body, and which was placed in the right hand in the hour of death, shows that she was a Christian child. And so in view of the evidence of Origen

[1] My sincere thanks are due to the following scholars: R. P. B. Couroyer, Jerusalem; Frl. M. Cramer, Münster; I. E. S. Edwards, London; W. Hengstenberg, Seeshaupt; P. Labib, Cairo; S. Morenz, Leipzig; E. Otto, Heidelberg; J. Spiegel, Göttingen; H. Stock, Cairo.
[2] J. Spiegel's expression.
[3] Cf. S. Morenz, 'Das Werden zu Osiris. Die Darstellungen auf einem Leinentuch der römischen Kaiserzeit (Berlin 11651) und verwandten Stücken', Staatliche Museen zu Berlin, Forschungen und Berichte I, Berlin, 1957, pp. 52–70.

about the practice of infant baptism in the Egyptian Church of that time, we must assume that the little girl was baptized.[1]

c. *Palestine*

For Palestine we have the important testimony of Origen. All the four writings in which he says that the baptism of παιδία/*parvuli* was an established practice of the Church,[2] which could be traced back to apostolic tradition, were written in Caesarea (Palestine).

d. *Syria*

If we turn lastly to Syria, we find that here practice in Eastern Syria was widely divergent from that in Western Syria. As we shall see in a moment,[3] it can be inferred from Origen that in Western Syria the general practice of the great Church with regard to infant baptism was followed. There is an indirectly confirmatory piece of evidence for the practice of infant baptism on the occasion of the conversion of heathen families, which is supplied to us by the *Pseudo-Clementines*. This evidence occurs in passages which must be ascribed to the original work which was composed in Western Syria about AD 220–230.[4]

Here the Apostle Peter is made to explain to Mattidia, the heathen mother of Clement, who has found her sons, whom she had believed to be dead, and who had in the interval become Christians, that a Christian cannot sit at table with a heathen so long as the latter is not baptized; and that this holds even for father, mother, wife, child, brother and relations.[5] This statement is expressly repeated to Faustus, the father of Clement, when he is recognized by his family; so long as he is unconverted he may not eat together with his *wife and children*.[6] Since it

---

[1] It may be noted in passing that this clay mummy coffin can claim special interest for quite a different reason. For it provides the earliest evidence of the use of the cross as a Christian symbol. Christian archaeology will have to revise its dogmatic judgment that the cross was not used as a Christian symbol until the age of Constantine, and admit that this was the case in Egypt as early as the third century. We saw that further the Egyptian tau-cross, the *ankh*-sign was, so to speak, its sponsor. In this also we can see Egyptian influence, for in this earliest piece of evidence we have to do with an amulet, which corresponds to a lotus-flower. (The crosses on the ossuaries found in Jerusalem's southern suburb, Talpioth, have nothing to do with Christian crosses; see E. Dinkler, 'Zur Geschichte des Kreuzsymbols', *ZTK* 48, 1951, pp. 148–72.)

[2] See above, pp. 65 f.

[3] See below, p. 70.

[4] E. Molland, 'La circoncision, le baptême, et l'autorité du décret apostolique (Actes XV 28sq.) dans les milieux judéo-Chrétiens des Pseudo-Clémentines', *ST* 9, 1955, pp. 1–39, here p. 22. On the dating of the original work cf. B. Rehm, *Die Pseudo-Clementinen* I: *Homilien* (*GCS* 42), Berlin 1953, p. VII.

[5] *Hom.* 13.4.4, par. *Recogn.* 7.29.

[6] *Hom.* 15.1.2, par. *Recogn.* 10.1–4.

is quite inconceivable that baptism in normal cases should have broken table-fellowship between parents and children, the result follows that in the *Pseudo-Clementines* the baptism of all children on the conversion of the parents is presupposed as customary and taken for granted.[1]

The first direct evidence for the practice of infant baptism in Syria is given by Asterius the Sophist (died after 341)[2] and the *Apostolic Constitutions* (370–80).[3]

In the case of Eastern Syria, there is no trace of evidence that here infant baptism was practised in the first centuries. This is not surprising when we reflect that the earliest history of Christianity in Edessa, Mesopotamia and Persia was very strongly marked by Marcionite influences.[4] In the Marcionite Church, baptism (and in the case of members coming over from the Great Church, re-baptism) and admission to the Lord's Supper were only granted to those who swore to remain unmarried, or if they were married vowed abstinence in marriage (Tertullian, *Adv. Marcionem* IV 11.8; 34.5 etc.).[5] The Church in Eastern Syria acted similarly in its earliest days.[6] As late as 343 the Synod of Gangra (Paphla-

---

[1] This conclusion is supported by the emphasis with which it is asserted in *Hom.* 13.21.2 f. that no ἀβάπτιστος can enter into the kingdom of God.

[2] See below, p. 93.

[3] See below, p. 92. My colleague, Dr W. Strothmann, has had the kindness to refer me in a letter of 11 April 1958 to two references to baptism in the (Syrian) letters of John the Hermit (beginning of the fifth century?): 'What profit have children from baptism?' (L. G. Rignell, *Briefe von Johannes dem Einsiedler*, Lund, 1941, p. 3); 'or what reasons can one have for bringing small children to baptism?' (*ibid.*, p. 13).

[4] W. Bauer, *Rechtgläubigkeit und Ketzerei im ältesten Christentum* (Beiträge zur Historischen Theologie 10), Tübingen, 1934, pp. 21 f., 27–34, 38, 40; A. Vööbus, *Celibacy, a Requirement for Admission to Baptism in the Early Syrian Church* (Papers of the Estonian Theological Society in Exile 1), Stockholm, 1951, pp. 13–16.

[5] Cf. F. C. Burkitt, *Early Eastern Christianity*, London, 1904, p. 136; A. von Harnack, *Marcion: Das Evangelium vom fremden Gott* (TU 45), Leipzig, 1921, pp. 101, 186 f. I owe this reference to my friend Hermann Dörries.

[6] F. C. Burkitt, *op. cit.*, pp. 118–55; K. Müller, *Die Forderung der Ehelosigkeit für alle Getauften in der alten Kirche* (Sammlung gemeinverständlicher Vorträge und Schriften aus dem Gebiet der Theologie und Religionsgeschichte 126), Tübingen, 1927, pp. 18 ff.; G. Richter, 'Über die älteste Auseinandersetzung der syrischen Christen mit den Juden', *ZNW* 35, 1936, pp. 110–14; E. J. Duncan, *Baptism in the Demonstrations of Aphraates the Persian Sage* (The Catholic University of America Studies in Christian Antiquity 8), Washington, 1945. Recently A. Vööbus has sifted the source-material in a fascinating and learned discussion. Like his predecessors, he came to the conclusion that the Eastern Syrian Church, under the influence of the Marcionites, the Valentinians and Tatian (pp. 13–17), demanded celibacy as a condition of baptism (pp. 21–34). But he has shown at the same time the untenability of Burkitt's view, that Aphraates in his homilies (337–45) still made the same claim. The passage in the seventh homily (337) which gives a contrary impression, is rather, on the opinion of Vööbus, supported by A. Baumstark, a quotation from an old baptismal liturgy (pp. 49–58). In fact the reaction which enjoined a relaxation of the ascetic practice in relation to baptism had already taken place by the time of Aphraates (p. 48).

gonia) had by solemn decree to condemn the supporters of Eustathius of Sebaste (Armenia) who demanded that when married persons joined the Church they should dissolve their marriage.[1] As we can infer from Canon 15, there were even cases of parents abandoning their children: 'If anyone deserts his children and does not bring them up and lead them as far as he can to a fitting piety, but neglects them under a pretence of asceticism, let him be anathema.' Where this gnostic ascetic Christianity was prevalent there was obviously no place for infant baptism.

At the close of this survey of the development in the eastern part of the Church up to the middle of the third century we must once more draw attention to the outstanding significance of the statements of Origen (see pp. 65 f.). What gives them such great importance is the wide outlook of this learned man. Not only was he born into an Egyptian family and lived till 231 in Egypt (Alexandria), not only do the five utterances we have cited belong to the time of his activities in Palestine (Caesarea) but, in addition, on his numerous journeys he visited Rome, Greece, Western Syria, Cappadocia and the parts of Arabia adjoining Palestine. He could not have talked in so unqualified a manner of infant baptism as 'the custom of the church' (*ecclesiae observantia*) if in his journeys he had come on deviations in practice within the sphere of the great Church. Thus his witness holds good for practically the whole eastern Church of his time.

2. THE WEST

A. *Greece*

Under Hadrian (117-138) Aristides of Athens wrote an *Apology* whose text has been known to us only since 1878 through an Armenian fragment (Chap. 1 f.), and in its entirety only since the discovery of the Syriac translation by J. R. Harris in 1889. The original Greek text is preserved at least partially in excerpts and papyrus fragments.[2] The more extensive first part of the *Apology* (1-14) is a polemic against the religions of the barbarians, Greeks and Jews, while the shorter second part (15-17) sets forth the Christian faith in contrast with them. This second part aims at the refutation of calumnies and therefore consciously plays down the element of dogma; the whole emphasis is laid on the exemplary character of Christian morality. At the beginning of the last chapter Aristides expressly emphasizes the fact that he has intentionally refrained from

---

[1] Canons 1, 9, 10, 14 (Hardouin I, 533 ff.; Lauchert, pp. 80 ff.).
[2] See the list of sources, p. 11.

entering into the detail of Christian doctrine: 'So much, O King, I purposed to explain, for about the rest, as has been said, words are to be found in their other writings which are much too difficult to be cited or repeated by anyone' (17.1).[1] Accordingly the sacraments are not mentioned, at least not directly.

What has been said must be borne in mind, if the passage 15.11 is to be rightly understood: 'And when a child is born to them *they thank God*; and if it die in infancy, they thank him exceedingly, because it departed this life sinless.'[2] We are concerned with the phrase printed in italics, 'they thank God' (εὐχαριστοῦσιν τῷ θεῷ, Syr. *mwdyn l'lh*). Aristides loves this phrase and uses it again in 15.10 to describe prayers in the morning and grace at meals.[3] In 15.11 it is twice used for the service at the death of a member of the Church,[4] and in addition in 17.4, where the writer says, 'And if it happens that one of them (the pagans) is converted, he is ashamed before the Christians of the things that he has done, and thanks God,[5] saying, "In ignorance have I done them." And he purifies his heart, and his sins are forgiven him.'[6] In this passage the expression 'to thank God' is a reference to baptism. Since Aristides always uses this expression to describe Christian rites, and since, as we saw, he does not mention baptism directly but only indicates it with the phrase 'thanks God', it is also very probable that here too in 15.11 when he uses the words, 'When a child is born to them they thank God,' he is referring to baptism. The sentence immediately following supports this conclusion. The special hymn of praise to God which the congregation raises at the burial of a little child 'because it departed this life "sinless"' (ἀναμάρτητον, 15.11) can hardly refer to the innocence of childhood, but much more probably to the forgiveness which is given in baptism. On consultation I see that so great an authority on the early Christian liturgies as Th. Schermann noted our passage—though without further explanation—as evidence for infant baptism.[7] It is clear that this indirect evidence can be evaluated only against the background of the other evidence.

---

[1] Harris, TS 1.1, Syriac, pp. 26.22–27.2 (translated on p. 51). Only the first words, down to 'king', are preserved in the Greek.

[2] Br. Mus. Gr. Pap. 2486, lines 39–42; Syriac, Harris, 25.7–10.

[3] Lines 33 f.; Syriac, 25.3 f.

[4] Lines 37 f.: χαίρουσιν καὶ εὐχαριστοῦσιν καὶ προσεύχονται περὶ αὐτοῦ; Syriac, p. 25.5 f.; see also line 41 cited above.

[5] Harris translates 'confess' (p. 51), but the Syriac (p. 27.15) is the same as above, *mwd' l'lh*.

[6] Syriac, p. 27.13–17; Greek wanting.

[7] Th. Schermann, *Die allgemeine Kirchenordnung, frühchristliche Liturgien und kirchliche Überlieferung* II. *Frühchristliche Liturgien* (Studien zur Geschichte und Kultur des Altertums, 3. Ergänzungsband, 2), Paderborn, 1915, p. 269 n. 2.

B. *Italy and Gaul*

Here the oldest witness takes us back to the time of the Gospel of John. In his *First Apology* (AD 150–55) Justin Martyr, whose sphere of activity was Rome, mentions 'many men and women of the age of sixty and seventy years who have been disciples of Christ from childhood (οἳ ἐκ παίδων ἐμαθητεύθησαν τῷ Χριστῷ)', and who had kept their Christian faith untarnished through a long life.[1] The passive of the word μαθητεύειν signifies 'becoming a Christian', *Dial.* 39.2, with clear reference to baptism.[2] The men and women mentioned by Justin were consequently baptized 'as children' (ἐκ παίδων) in the time between AD 80 and 95.

To the period before AD 150[3] belongs a correction made in the Western recension of the text of Acts 2.39. Here in the oldest text, which gives the reasons underlying the demand for baptism, the reading was, 'For the promise is to you and to your children.'[4] Now D d Aug. read: 'For the promise is to us and to our children.' Thus the statement is now made to refer to Christian children.[5] Now we must be careful not to base too far-reaching conjectures on a variant reading, but on the other hand we must not simply ignore it, as is usually done. The most natural explanation of the variant is that the formulation 'Be baptized every one of you . . . for the promise is to us and our children' came naturally to the redactor's pen, because the baptism of Christian children was a custom taken for granted.

The next witness, Irenaeus of Lyons (born between 130 and 140), the most important theologian of the second century AD, writes soon after 180: 'For he (Jesus) has come to save all of them by himself: all those, I say, who through him are reborn into God, infants, young children, boys, the mature and older people' (*omnes enim venit (Jesus) per semetipsum salvare :*

---

[1] *Apol.* I 15.6

[2] . . . μαθητευομένους εἰς τὸ ὄνομα τοῦ Χριστοῦ αὐτοῦ . . . φωτιζόμενοι διὰ τοῦ ὀνόματος τοῦ Χριστοῦ τούτου. Cf. Ph.-H. Menoud, 'Le baptême des enfants dans l'Église ancienne', *Verbum Caro* 2, 1948, p. 19; W. F. Flemington, *The New Testament Doctrine of Baptism*, p. 132.

[3] J. H. Ropes, *The Text of Acts* (third volume of *The Beginnings of Christianity*: I: *The Acts of the Apostles*, ed. F. J. Foakes Jackson and K. Lake), London, 1926, p. ccxxiii (cf. ccxl): The Western Text of the Acts dates from 'before the middle of the second century'. This date is confirmed by the consideration that the unusually free manner in which the western recension of the Acts handles the text, is only conceivable in the time before this book, 'in the last third of the second century', became a regularly read scripture of the Church (Martin Dibelius, *Studies in the Acts of the Apostles*, ET London, 1956, p. 90).

[4] See above, pp. 40 f.

[5] D. Plooij, 'The ascension in the "Western" textual tradition', *Mededeelingen der Koninklijke Akademie van Wetenschappen te Amsterdam, Afdeeling Letterkunde*, 67 A, 1929 (no. 2), pp. 39–58, here p. 53; H. Windisch, 'Zum Problem der Kindertaufe im Urchristentum', *ZNW* 28, 1929, p. 122 n. 2.

omnes, inquam, qui per eum renascuntur in Deum, infantes et parvulos et pueros et iuvenes et seniores).[1] Irenaeus in the preceding words opposes the gnostic belief that Christ descended upon the man Jesus, and insists that Jesus was Christ from his birth. This statement is important for Irenaeus because it leads to the conclusion that Jesus sanctifies and saves every age, babies and little children as well as boys, youths and older men, in short, 'all who through him are reborn into God' (*renascuntur in Deum*). Since Irenaeus, following the fully established and quite unvarying terminology of the Church,[2] describes baptism as 'regeneration into God' (*regeneratio in Deum*),[3] he bears witness in our passage to infant baptism and presupposes it as 'an unquestioned practice of the Church'.[4]

Still more important than the sources mentioned above is the *Apostolic Tradition* of Hippolytus. The ascription of the so-called *Egyptian Church Order* to Hippolytus by E. Schwartz in 1910[5] and R. H. Connolly in 1916[6] is of great importance for our theme. For thereby this work is given the same outstanding significance for the West as evidence for infant baptism, as we saw the evidence of Origen to possess for the East. It is true that its investigation is still in many respects in the early stages. Our first objective must be the attempt to restore the original Greek text, lost except for small fragments. We know it only through the translations and re-workings mentioned above on pp. 13 f., which, however, differ considerably from one another. The various strands of the complex tradition have not yet all been sufficiently examined to allow a reconstruction of the original text in all particulars.[7] All the more

---

[1] *Adv. Haer.* II 33.2 (Harvey)=II 22.4 (*MPG* 7).

[2] John 3.5; Tit. 3.5; Justin, *Apol.* I 61.3 f.,10; 66.1; *Dial.* 138.2; *Orac. Sib.* VIII 316; *Acts of Thomas* 132; Clement of Alexandria, *Paedagogus* I 25.1–3 (*MPG* 8, 280); *Excerpta ex Theodoto* 80.1; Origen, *Hom. in Luke* XXVIII; *Comm. on John*, Frag. 121; *Pseudo-Clem. Hom.* 7.8.1; 11.26.1 f.; 11.27.2 and very frequently. 'All the antient Christians, not one Man excepted, do take the Word *Regeneration* or *new Birth* to signifie Baptism: and *regenerate*, baptized' (W. Wall, *The History of Infant Baptism* II, London 1705, p. 365).

[3] *Adv. Haer.* I 14.1; III 18.1; V 15.3 (Harvey)=I 21.1; III 17.1; V 15.3 (*MPG* 7); *Demonstr.* 3.7.

[4] H. Windisch, *op. cit.*, p. 135; cf. Ph.-H. Menoud, *op. cit.*, pp. 20 f. So also Th.-A. Audet, 'Orientations théologiques chez Saint Irénée. Le Contexte mental d'une *ΓΝΩΣΙΣ ΑΛΗΘΗΣ*', *Traditio* I, New York, 1943, pp. 15–54, here p. 18 n. 6; J.-C. Didier, 'Un cas typique de développement du dogme. A propos du baptême des enfants', *MelScR* 9, 1952, p. 196; recently T. F. Torrance, 'Ein vernachlässigter Gesichtspunkt der Tauflehre: 4. Die Lehre des Irenaeus', *Evangelische Theologie* 16, 1956, pp. 481–92.

[5] *Über die pseudoapostolischen Kirchenordnungen* (Schriften der Wissenschaftlichen Gesellschaft in Strassburg 6), Strassburg, 1910.

[6] *The So-called Egyptian Church Order and Derived Documents* (TS 8.4), Cambridge, 1916.

[7] Of the sources cited on pp. 13 f., the Arabic version of the *Church Order* was made available to the public as early as 1912 by J. and A. Périer, *Les '127 Canons des Apôtres'* (Patrologia Orientalis 8.4), Paris, 1912. A comprehensive critical edition of the

important is the agreement of the tradition in the section mentioning infant baptism (see below, p. 75 n. 1), which allows us to conclude with certainty that we have in this passage the original version of Hippolytus' *Apostolic Tradition*. It is of the greatest significance that we should thus get an insight into the baptismal practice of Rome in the second half of the second century. It is true that the *Apostolic Tradition*, as far as its composition goes, must be dated to about 215, but its material is older and it would actually be a mistake if we were to reckon the work merely as evidence for the beginning of the third century. For Hippolytus, who probably incorporated the Church Order into his book περὶ χαρισμάτων ἀποστολικὴ παράδοσις as its second part, had no intention of introducing new rules for church action, but as the title of his work indicates, of setting down the older ('apostolic') tradition. And this is true also of infant baptism.

Hippolytus' Order of Service for the rite of baptism begins with the words 'At cock-crow let prayers first be said over the water' (21). From this indication of time we must infer that Hippolytus has in mind the great festival for the baptism of converts on Easter morning.[1] The order of procedure was as follows: first the children were baptized, including the smallest children who could not yet speak (i.e. answer the baptismal questions), for which reason their parents or a relative answered for

---

Ethiopic has been published by H. Duensing, *Der aethiopische Text der Kirchenordnung des Hippolyt* (Abhandlungen der Akademie der Wissenschaften in Göttingen, Phil.-hist. Klasse III 32), Göttingen, 1946, and one of the important Coptic version by W. Till and J. Leipoldt in 1954 (but compare this with the discussions of L. Th. Lefort, *Le Muséon* 67, 1954, pp. 403–5, and B. Botte, *Bulletin de Théologie ancienne et médiévale* 7, 1955, pp. 26 f.). On the state of the investigation cf. B. Botte, 'Le texte de la *Tradition apostolique*', *Recherches de Théologie ancienne et médiévale* 22, 1955, pp. 161–72. G. Dix, Ἀποστολικὴ παράδοσις: *The Treatise on the Apostolic Tradition of St Hippolytus of Rome* I, London, 1937, and B. Botte, *Hippolyte de Rome. La Tradition Apostolique* (SC 11), Paris, 1946, have attempted a provisional general reconstruction from all the sources available to them. Cf. also the work of Th. Schermann (see p. 71 n. 7), and E. Hennecke, *Neutestamentliche Apokryphen*², Tübingen, 1924, pp. 569–83.

[1] Cf. O. Casel, 'Art und Sinn der ältesten christlichen Osterfeier', *Jahrbuch für Liturgiewissenschaft* 14, 1938, pp. 1–78; here p. 23; J. Jeremias, 'πάσχα', *TWNT* V, 1954, p. 902 nn. 57 f.; Tertullian, *De Baptismo* (200/206) 19.1: *diem baptismo sollemniorem pascha praestat*; Hippolytus of Rome, *Commentary on Daniel* (about 204) I 16.2 (*GCS* Hippol. I 1, p. 26); Methodius of Olympus (died 311), *Symposium* VIII 6 (*GCS* 27, p. 88). From the Decretal of Pope Siricius to Himerius of Tarragona of 10 February 385 (see below, p. 94 n. 5), we know that it was an old Roman custom to baptize adults only at Easter, and in the season of rejoicing between then and Pentecost, exception being made only in the case of little children and people whose life was in danger. Canon 7 of the Synod of Rome (402) also confirms Easter baptism as the normal thing for Rome and Gaul (Hardouin I 1035 f.). Egeria, *Peregrinatio ad loca sancta* 38.1 (Itinera Hierosolymitana saec. IIII–VIII, *CSEL* 39, p. 90; SC 21, pp. 238 f.) does the same for Jerusalem and Spain. Evidence from individual inscriptions for converts' baptism at Easter, *ILCV* I 1539 (AD 338, about 30 years old); *ILCV* I 1541 (AD 463, about 6 years old). Augustine was baptized on Easter Eve, 387.

them; then the grown men were baptized, and lastly the women (21.3 ff.). Thus what we see happening is in fact the accession of 'households' to the Christian fellowship. The passage which deals with the baptism of children runs thus, according to the Coptic text: 'First you should baptize the little ones. All who can speak for themselves should speak. But for those who cannot speak, their parents should speak or another who belongs to their family' (21.3 f.).[1] We see that Hippolytus accepts infant baptism as an 'unquestioned rule'[2] which needs no justification; the probationary period of three years prescribed in *Apostolic Tradition* 17 before baptism is omitted in the case of children.

At least as important as the actual statement contained in Hippolytus' work and its preceding history is its influence on later times; as we shall see, it was not only translated into Latin but, most important of all, into the most diverse oriental languages, and served as a foundation for numerous Church Orders in subsequent times. Thus it became during the next centuries the normative order for the administration of baptism in a great part of the Church.

The witness of the literary texts for the practice of infant baptism in Italy and Gaul in the first Christian centuries receives valuable confirmation from inscriptions. We give below some epitaphs from the third century (mostly Roman) of small children who had been baptized, noting in passing that there are no Christian epitaphs earlier than AD 200.[3] But as soon as the era of Christian inscriptions begins, we find evidence also for infant baptism.[4]

In the third century there are many attributes and symbols in the tombstone inscriptions of little children, which allow us to infer that we

[1] Funk ch. 16: Till-Leipoldt, 19. The Ethiopic text (Duensing 55) agrees word for word with the Coptic, the Arabic (Périer-Périer 602 [52] f.) almost exactly, *Test. Dom.* II 8 (Rahmani 127) and *Can. Hippol.* 19.7 (Riedel 211) in essentials.

[2] A. von Harnack, *Die Mission und Ausbreitung des Christentums in den ersten drei Jahrhunderten* I[4], Leipzig 1924, p. 399 n. 2.

[3] A. M. Schneider, 'Die ältesten Denkmäler der Römischen Kirche', *Festschrift zur Feier des Zweihundertjährigen Bestehens der Akademie der Wissenschaften in Göttingen* II, phil.-hist. Klasse, Berlin-Göttingen-Heidelberg, 1951, p. 166: 'Neither archaeology nor epigraphy—in spite of the most extensive investigations—has succeeded in disclosing even one Christian monument that could be dated with certainty earlier than 200.' That is true even of Rome (p. 190). Even if the *Sator-Arepo* formula of Pompeii (G. de Jerphanion, 'La formule magique Sator Arepo ou Rotas Opera', *Recherches de Science Religieuse* 25, 1935, pp. 196 ff.) is believed (and rightly so in my opinion) to be a Christian inscription of a date earlier than AD 79, Schneider's judgment is absolutely true as far as tombstone inscriptions are concerned.

[4] Only the expert can fully understand how this book has been enriched by my being able to count upon the unfailing and unselfish help of my late friend and colleague in the Göttingen Academy, A. M. Schneider, in the collection and dating of inscriptions.

are dealing with baptized children. The following inscription is as early as approximately AD 200 or shortly afterwards:[1]

```
EVTYCHIANO
FIl.IO·DVLCISSIMO
EV ГYCHVS·PATER·
D·L·VA·I·M·II D·IIII
DEI·SERVS·I⳩·
    IXΘYC
```

Tombstone inscription of the child Eutychianus

Eutychiano
filio dulcissimo
Eutychus pater
d(e)d(icauit) u(ixit) a (nno) I m(ensibus) II d(iebus) IIII
5 *Dei ser(u)us* Ἰ(ησοῦς) Χρ(ιστός)
   Ἰ(ησοῦς) Χ(ριστὸς) Θ(εοῦ) Υ(ἱὸς) Σ(ωτήρ)[2]

By the predicate *Dei ser(u)us* ('slave of God') the one-year-old child is marked as baptized.[3]

A similar predicate (Χρειστοῦ δοῦλος, 'slave of Christ') is given to the 'holy infant' (ἁγνὸν παιδίον) Kyriakos, mentioned on another inscription belonging to the third century.

   Κυριακὸς Χρεισ
   τοῦ δοῦλος
   ἁγνὸν παιδί
   ον ἐνθάδε κεῖτε
5   μνησκόμενοι γονεῖς Διονύ
   σιος καὶ Ζωσίμη τέκνων γλυ
   κυτάτῳ ἐποιήσαμεν[4]

---

[1] Dölger, *Ichthys* I², p. 197.
[2] *ILCV* I 1611 C; Dölger, *op. cit.*, pp. 192–97, Rome.
[3] Dölger, *op. cit.*, p. 195.   [4] *CIG* IV 564, no. 9801; Kraft 35, Rome.

The fragment of a metrical tombstone inscription which mentions baptism (*lavacro*) belongs to the grave of a child who died at a very early age (it is addressed as *dulcissime nate*).[1]

We have mentioned already on p. 56 Zosimus, πιστὸς ἐκ πιστῶν, and the three boys called πιστοὶ γενετῇ.

The 'innocent infant' (νήπιος ἄκακος) Dionysios is described as baptized by the phrase 'He lies here with the holy ones'(ἐνθάδε κεῖτε μετὰ τῶν ἁγίων):

> Διονύσιος νήπιος
> ἄκακος ἐνθάδε κεῖ
> τε μετὰ τῶν ἁ
> γίων μνήσκεσθε
> 5 δὲ καὶ ἡμῶν ἐν ταῖ
> ς ἁγίαις ὑμῶν πρ(οσ)ευχα(ῖ)ς
> καὶ τοῦ γλύψα(ν)τος καὶ γράψαν
> τος[2]

⟨Leaf, anchor⟩ ⟨Dove on branch, leaf⟩

In the case of the two-year-old Pomponia Fortunata the phrase 'she died in peace' (*decesset* [=*decessit*] *in pace*) and the symbol of the fish indicates baptism, and the symbol makes it possible to date the inscription in the third century.[3]

> *d(is) m(anibus)*
> *Pomponiae Fortuna*
> *tae que decesset in pace*
> *que uixit ann(os) II m(ensem) I dies XV*
> ⟨fish⟩[4]

In the case of the three-year-old Innocens baptism is to be inferred from the formula *spirito sancto* which probably also indicates the third century:

> *spirito sancto*
> *Innocenti qui*
> *uixit an(nos) pl(us) m(inus) III*[5]

On account of the opening words A. M. Schneider would, with some reserve, also ascribe to the third century the following inscription about a baptized (*te cum pace*) child almost a year old.

> [. . . *Sabi?*] *niane te cum pace*
> [*annum vi*] *xit XI dies minus*
> [*et no*] *n suplebit XI di*ϵ*s*[6] *at annu(m)*[7]

Furthermore, the combination of Latin text with Greek lettering

[1] *ILCV* I 1520; Dölger, *op. cit.*, pp. 198 f. Place of origin unknown, now in Rome. For the dating of the inscription in the third century, cf. Dölger, *op. cit.*, p. 199.
[2] *CIG* IV 527, no. 9574; Kraft 36, Rome.
[3] Information from A. M. Schneider.
[4] *ILCV* II 3891 C, Rome, St Callisto.   [5] *ILCV* II 3394 A, Rome.
[6] *Sic*, with a Greek ϵ.
[7] *ILCV* II 2264, Rome. At the side a large ivy.

in the next two inscriptions certainly indicates a date in the third century. The symbol gives grounds for inferring that Theodora, who died at the age of eleven months, was baptized, and the words ιν πακε in the inscription of the two-year-old Alexandria necessitate a similar conclusion:

⟨Traces of a jar⟩
βενε μερεντι φιλιε
Θεοδωρε κυε βιξιτ
μησις XI διης[1] XVII
XVII ⟨Bird with twig in beak⟩[2]

[Αλεξ]ανδρια δουκις (= dulcis)
κε βιξιτ annis II
[μ]ινας II qu[iescit]
ιν πακε[3]

Four Roman inscriptions of the third century on children's tombs form a group by themselves. They explicitly mention the time of the date of baptism, since it was administered when the child in question was at the point of death. The first of these inscriptions, which tells of the one-and-three-quarter-year-old Apronianus, was already discussed on pp. 41 f. The Tyche inscription[4] also deals with the baptism in emergency of a small child. Like the Apronianus inscription it was found in the Priscilla Catacomb in Rome:

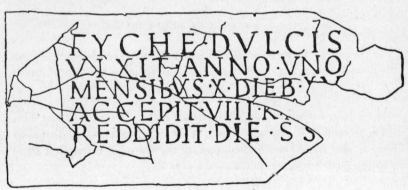

Tombstone inscription of the child Tyche

Tyche dulcis
uixit anno uno
mensibus X dieb(us) XV
accepit[5] VIII k[. . .
5   reddidit[6] die s(upra) s(cripto)[7]

[1] Sic, with a Latin d.   [2] ILCV II 4464. Now in Rome.   [3] ILCV II 4469, Rome.
[4] On its ascription to the third century, cf. Dölger, Ichthys II 521.
[5] Sc. gratiam, i.e. baptism.   [6] Sc. spiritum.   [7] ILCV I 1531; Kraft 36.

Since the day of baptism is the same as the day of death it was undoubtedly an emergency baptism which little Tyche received at the age of one year, ten months and fifteen days.

From the Priscilla Catacomb also comes the Irene inscription.[1]

Tombstone inscription of the child Irene

Ir[en]e quae uix(it)
cum p[are]ntibus
suis m(ensibus) XI d(iebus) VI
acc(epit)[2] VII id. April
5 *et redd(idit)[3] id. A[p]ril[4]*

The little child Irene was thus baptized on the day in which she was eleven months old; since baptism (7 April) was received six days before her death, one would naturally think in this case also of an emergency baptism.[5] On the other hand, considering the day of baptism (7 April) it might be a normal baptism on Easter Day, where the families of converts were baptized.[6] But these alternatives are not necessarily mutually exclusive. It might perhaps have happened that the illness of the little child who, as is so touchingly said, 'lived with her parents 11 months 6 days', gave them the impulse to ask for baptism, which the little Irene survived by only six days. But this combination is of course pure conjecture and we regret once more that the inscriptions are so reticent.

The fourth inscription of the third century which deals with an emergency baptism gives the date. It comes from the year 268 (Rome) and tells of the baptism of a twelve-year-old boy, Marcianus, which obviously

---

[1] On its ascription to the third century, cf. Dölger, *loc. cit.*
[2] Sc. *gratiam*, i.e. baptism.
[3] Sc. *spiritum.*   [4] *ILCV* I 1532; Kraft 36.
[5] So Dölger, *Ichthys* II 524.
[6] On baptism at Easter see above, p. 74. In this case the inscription could be dated; according to A. M. Schneider it would fall in the year 251 or 261.

(the inscription is injured just at this place, but its completion is hardly in doubt) was administered on his death-bed, one day before his death.

> Pasto [r et T]i[t]iana et ⟨Dove⟩ Marciana et ⟨Leaf⟩
> Chr[e]st[e Mar]ciano filio benemerenti [in]
> Χρ. dn. fec[eru]n[t] qui uixit annus XII m(enses) II et d[ies . . .]
> qui cra [tiam]¹ accepit d. n. die XII ka[l.O]ctob[r]es [Ma]
> 5 [rini]ano (et) Paterno II coss. et rede [dit]² XI ka[l. ss?]
> uibas (=vivas) inter sanctis in a[eternum]³

Since the patristic sources of the third century, especially Origen and Cyprian, give us to understand that the children of Christian parents were baptized in infancy, and since the first certain instance of the delay of baptism in the case of the children of Christian parents belongs to 329–30,[4] we must conclude that these emergency baptisms were administered to children of non-Christians. The inscriptions themselves, so far as they permit of conjecture, confirm this conclusion. We saw already, on p. 42, that the father of the little boy Apronianus, baptized on the urgent appeal of the Christian grandmother, was almost certainly a pagan, and in the case of the little Irene, the date of baptism (April 7) made a similar assumption possible.

Scanty though the information may be from the inscriptions in each individual case relating to the persons of the dead children, yet when the whole mosaic is pieced together, the picture is a rich one. They fall into two groups. In the first group of baptized children only the age of the child at death is mentioned, usually in numbers, but occasionally instead in descriptive terms such as *dulcissimus natus* (see p. 77), νήπιος ἄκακος (ibid.), ἀγνὸν παιδίον (see p. 76). From these descriptions it can be seen that at least in these cases baptism was administered in infancy, which indicates Christian parents. Twice (with the phrase πιστὸς ἐκ πιστῶν or πιστοὶ γενετῇ, see pp. 55 f.) the Christian status of the parents is directly mentioned. In the second group the date of the baptism is mentioned along with the child's age; in all these cases we have to do with baptism *in extremis*. The children of this group were of different ages at the time of baptism, from eleven months to twelve years old. In all probability in these cases the parents were pagan. Thus the literary witness of the second and third centuries, which supplies a relatively rich amount of evidence for infant baptism, receives varied illustration from the tombstone inscriptions.

¹ i.e. baptism.   ² Sc. *spiritum*.   ³ *ILCV* II 3315. Rome, St Callisto.
⁴ See below, pp. 88 f.

C. *Africa*

It is not until the year 180 that 'the church history of North Africa begins',[1] although the beginnings of Christianity in Africa must be earlier. We must hold this date in mind in order to evaluate correctly the fact that only twenty years later Tertullian expresses himself on the baptism of little children (*parvuli*).

With Tertullian's *De Paenitentia* we come for the first time upon a phenomenon which will have to concern us later—i.e. upon the tendency to postpone joining the Church, because of the belief that in view of the forgiveness to be expected in baptism one could continue in sin until baptism without worrying. Tertullian emphatically opposed this tendency.[2] It is all the more astonishing when we hear that in his book *De Baptismo* (ch. 18), composed in the same years (between 200 and 206), he advocated, admittedly from quite different motives, postponement of baptism in special cases, namely those of children and unmarried people. Like the exegetes of his time he does indeed understand the word of Jesus 'Forbid them not to come unto me' (Matt. 19.14) as an instruction of Jesus to baptize the children, but he has his doubts about too early an age. The baptism of little children (*parvuli*), he argues, except in cases of emergency baptism (*si non tamen necesse est*), lays too great a responsibility on the godparents; they might themselves die and consequently not be able to fulfil their promises, or bad tendencies (in their godchildren) might disclose themselves. For these reasons he advocates postponement. 'In every application for baptism the applicant can deceive himself and others. Therefore it is more expedient (*utilior*) with an eye on the condition and maturity of the person concerned, and also taking his age into consideration, to postpone baptism, especially when we have to deal with little children (*parvuli*). For what is the necessity (when there is no emergency) of endangering the godparents also who might themselves be hindered by death from the keeping of their promises, or else deceived by the manifestation of bad tendencies (in their godchildren)? It is true that the Lord says, "Forbid them not to come unto me." Very well, then, let them "come" when they are bigger (*dum adolescunt*), they may "come" when they (can) learn, when they are (able to be) instructed whither they should "come"; they may become Christians when they can know Christ. Why does the age of innocence need to be in such a hurry to receive forgiveness of sins (*quid festinat*

[1] A. von Harnack, *Die Mission und Ausbreitung des Christentums in den ersten drei Jahrhunderten* II⁴, Leipzig 1924, p. 891 (ET, *The Mission and Expansion of Christianity* II², London 1908, p. 277).   [2] *De Paenitentia* 6.3–24.

F

innocens aetas ad remissionem peccatorum)? In worldly matters one will proceed more cautiously; how should divine things be entrusted to some-one to whom earthly things cannot yet be entrusted? They should (at least) be in a position to strive after salvation, for you to be justified in believing that you have given it to one who is striving after it.' At the same time, on similar grounds, because of the responsibility which baptism lays upon us (*pondus baptismi*), Tertullian advises the postpone-ment of baptism in the case of unmarried persons, especially virgins and those recently widowed, whom he regards as exposed to special tempta-tions, 'until they either marry or make up their minds to continence'. At the same time Tertullian speaks about the day of baptism: 'The most solemn day for baptism is Easter, for on that day was fulfilled the Passion of the Lord, into which we are baptized.'[1]

In order to understand this passage we must take into account that the tract *De Baptismo*, like so many other tracts of Tertullian, was written to meet a special occasion. It seems to have had its origin in addresses to Carthaginian catechumens and neophytes.[2] This means, however, that in the whole tract Tertullian has primarily the baptism of converts in view. This conclusion is confirmed by several statements in the section quoted above. The very first sentence of the above passage mentions the *parvuli* in one breath with the candidates offering themselves as converts. And when the last sentence of our excerpt describes Easter as the most solemn day for baptism, we remember that, as we have already seen on p. 74, Easter was the time when families joining the Church were bap-tized. Further, confirmation is added by the undoubted fact that the *innupti* (virgins and widows) whom Tertullian mentions along with the *parvuli*, and in whose case he recommends a postponement of baptism, were pagan women joining the Church. And lastly, the mention of the godparents, who under the description *sponsores* appear in our passage for the first time in Christian literature, provides confirmation of the fact that Tertullian is thinking of missionary baptism. The institution of godparents was not confined to North Africa; on the contrary, in order to understand the 'sureties' of Tertullian we shall have to remember that almost at the same time the *Apostolic Tradition* of Hippolytus (about 215),[3] and later the *Apostolic Constitutions* (370/380)[4] and the *Testamentum Domini* (fifth century)[5] speak of persons who bear witness to the previous life of the applicants for baptism, on the occasion of their offering them-

[1] *De Baptismo* 18.3-19.1.
[2] R. F. Refoulé and M. Drouzy, *Tertullian: Traité du baptême* (SC 35), Paris, 1952, p. 11.
[3] 20.2.   [4] VIII 32.2.   [5] II 1.

selves as candidates for instruction, and that Egeria repeatedly speaks of
patres and *matres*, who give in the names of the catechumens and accom-
pany them during the time of their catechumenate.[1] These witnesses to
character who stood surety for pagans on the occasion of their applying
for baptismal instruction, seem in North Africa, as *De Baptismo* 18
implies, to have had an additional special function in the case of *parvuli*,
inasmuch as they acted for them as sureties (*sponsores*) and made
promises (*promissiones*) for them. By these promises appear to have
been understood the taking of the baptismal vows by the sponsor as
representative, whereby he undertook to care for the Christian education
of the child.[2]

The doubts expressed by Tertullian about child baptism—that an
unfair responsibility is being laid on the godparents and that the *innocens
aetas* does not yet require forgiveness of sins—refer, accordingly, to the
children of pagans joining the Church. They do not in principle contest
the legitimacy, but only the expediency, of their baptism: *cunctatio
baptismi utilior est*.[3] This is established without any doubt by the fact
that Tertullian expressly makes exception in the case of danger of death
(*si non tam necesse est*).[4] Further, his doubts did not extend to the baptism
of Christian children, as is shown by an utterance of his which we shall
discuss in a moment, where the impulsive and changeable man expresses
himself quite otherwise than in our passage about the 'age of innocence'
(*innocens aetas*).

But with all this we have not yet named the decisive fact for the pur-
pose of our investigation. It is this: Tertullian's reservations with reference to the baptism of little children on the occasion of their parents' conversion are directed against an established usage. That follows with
complete certainty from the fact that it was, as we saw, a regular part
of the baptismal ritual that godparents at the baptism of infants (*parvuli*)
stood surety for their future way of life. Nay more, Tertullian informs us
which scriptural passages were appealed to as authorizing child baptism,
namely, 'Forbid them not to come to me' (*nolite illos prohibere ad me*

---

[1] 45.2: *et sic adducuntur unus et unus conpetens; si uiri sunt cum patribus suis uenient,
si autem feminae cum matribus suis,* cf. 46.1.5. Further references in E. Dick, 'Das
Pateninstitut im altchristlichen Katechumenat', *Zeitschrift für katholische Theologie* 63,
1939, pp. 1–49, here pp. 5,11.

[2] In Rome the parents 'or another, who belongs to their family' (Hippol., *Apost.
Trad.* 21.4), took the baptismal oath as representative of the child. E. Dick, in the essay
just mentioned, rightly emphasizes that a sharp distinction must be drawn between
the witnesses to character mentioned above ('Katechumenatszeugen') and the assistants
at baptism (mostly deacons or deaconesses). But he is hardly right when he dis-
tinguishes sharply between 'Katechumenatszeugen' and *sponsores*.

[3] *De Baptismo* 18.4.   [4] *Ibid.*

venire, Matt. 19.14)[1] and 'Give to every one who begs from you' (*omni petenti te dato*, Luke 6.30).[2] Thus right at the beginning of the North African Church we find infant baptism as a universally observed practice.

In his writing *De Anima*, which already belongs to his Montanist period and was composed between 210 and 213,[3] Tertullian touched again on our theme. In chs. 39.3–40.1 he expounds I Cor. 7.14 as follows: 'Therefore [since in every man either by nature or because of heathen practices at his birth, there is a 'demoniac spirit'] practically no birth is pure, especially in the case of pagans (39.4). This enables us to understand the Apostle's assertion that the children of a mixed marriage are holy, both because of their descent from a Christian parent (*tam ex seminis praerogativa*), and also because of their (future) education in Christian doctrine (*quam ex institutionis*[4] *disciplina*).[5] 'Otherwise,' he says, 'they would be born impure' (I Cor. 7.14). He meant his readers to understand that the sons (=children) of believers were in a sense marked out for holiness and therewith for salvation; through the pledge of this hope he wished to protect the marriages for whose preservation he was pleading. In addition he had the Lord's declaration in mind: 'Unless a man be born of water and the spirit he cannot enter into the kingdom of God' (John 3.5), i.e. he cannot be holy (40.1). Thus every soul is enrolled in Adam until it is enrolled anew in Christ; it is impure until it is enrolled anew; and because impure, sinful, responsible also for the stain of the flesh with which it is united.' While in the first passage quoted (*De Baptismo* 18) Tertullian had spoken of the children of pagans joining the Church, he is speaking in our passage of the 'children of believers' including the children of mixed marriages. Of them he says that by their birth they are 'marked out for holiness and therewith for salvation'; they are however, according to John 3.5 only made holy by baptism (39.4). Until baptism their soul is in Adam (and consequently burdened with original sin) and impure (40.1). Clearly Tertullian here

---

[1] 18.5.

[2] 18.1; cf. J.-C. Didier, 'Un cas typique de développement du dogme. A propos du baptême des enfants', *MelScR* 9, 1952, pp. 196 f.

[3] J. H. Waszink, pp. 5* f.

[4] *Institutio* = 'the body of teaching given by the Church of Rome' (both doctrine and practice), cf. V. Morel, 'Le développement de la "disciplina" sous l'action du Saint-Esprit chez Tertullien', *Revue d'Histoire Ecclésiastique* 35, 1939, pp. 253 f.

[5] The word *disciplina* would appear next to *ratio* to be the noun most used in Tertullian; he uses it 320 times. The many shades of meaning with which he uses the word have been elucidated by V. Morel, *op. cit.*, pp. 243–65; 'Disciplina, le mot et l'idée représentée par lui dans les oeuvres de Tertullian', *op. cit.*, vol. 40, 1944–45, pp. 5–46; 'Disciplina', *RAC* III, 1957, cols. 1213–29. According to Morel *disciplina* means: 1. 'instruction', 2. 'education', 'rules imposed', 'observation of these rules'.

does not only presuppose the practice of infant baptism,[1] but he advocates it.[2] The reservations expressed in *De Baptismo* 18 were not extended by Tertullian to cover the baptism of the children of Christian parents; perhaps he had gone so far as to drop them altogether.

Tertullian's objections made no impression, not even upon Cyprian of Carthage who was in other respects so strongly influenced by him. How firmly established a custom infant baptism continued to be in North Africa is shown by a synod held in Carthage (251 or 253), which was confronted by the opinion of Bishop Fidus that, as with circumcision, baptism should not (except in cases of necessity) be administered until the eighth day after birth. But even this very early date seemed unacceptable to the sixty-seven bishops, men representing the whole of Christian Africa. We know of their unanimous decision from the sixty-fourth letter of Cyprian; because of original sin baptism should not be delayed till the eighth day, but the children should be baptized directly after birth ('on the second or third day').[3] From Cyprian's work *De Lapsis*, composed in 251, we further learn that it was even customary to admit little children to communion, which of course presupposes that they were baptized.[4]

That in cases of danger to life baptism was not postponed till the second or third day, as the Synod of Carthage had legislated for normal cases, but was administered immediately after birth, is shown by an inscription of the third century from Hadrumetum in North Africa:

> *Arisus i[n] pace*
> *natus ora sexta*
> *bixit s(upra) s(criptas) VIIII*[5]

From the words *in pace* ('in peace') we may infer that the little child who died nine hours after its birth was baptized.

The same phrasing recurs in another inscription which probably also belongs to the third century, coming from Mactari in Africa:

> *d(is) m(anibus) s(acrum)*
> *bisis (=vixit) me(nse)s*
> *oto minus*
> *zis (=dies sex) Baduma*
> *s in pa(ce)*[6]

---

[1] H. Windisch, 'Zum Problem der Kindertaufe im Urchistentum', *ZNW* 28, 1929, p. 136.

[2] Windisch, *op. cit.*, pp. 135 f.; A. Oepke, 'Urchristentum und Kindertaufe', *ZNW* 29, 1930, pp. 88 f. [3] *Ep.* 64.2.

[4] *De Lapsis* 9; see also the vividly described special case, ch. 25.

[5] *ILCV* II 4429 A.

[6] *ILCV* II 3943. The *Acts of Crispina* (martyred AD 295 in Thebeste, North Africa,

If we survey the whole of the material set forth in this chapter it becomes evident that the individual pieces of evidence have varying weight. The statements of Origen, Hippolytus and Tertullian, which all carry us back into the second century, are of outstanding importance; they constitute the scaffolding which supports the rest of the evidence. It is further to be noted that the distribution of the evidence is very uneven; the West supplies us with much more material than the more reticent East. And yet in general the picture is the same. Everywhere, with the exception of Eastern Syria, we find in the second century infant baptism as an old and established usage of the Great Church, which both East and West agree in tracing back to the apostles. The evidence applies equally to children of Christian and pagan parents; Tertullian alone made a difference between the two groups; his advice to postpone the baptism of children referred to the children of pagan parents and to them alone. Nowhere was there any ground adduced for the postponement of the baptism of children of Christian parents, not even in Tertullian. On the contrary the East and the West, as far as our information extends, are unanimous in naming the age of infancy (Irenaeus), more precisely the first days after birth (Origen, Cyprian) as the age for baptism. The inscriptions, which begin in the West about 200, confirm in detail the picture supplied by the literary sources.

in the persecution of Diocletian), make the martyred woman say (2.1): *hoc* (sacrifice) *non feci aliquando ex quo nata sum, nec novi nec facio usquequo vixero.* At the end of the trial (3.3), she says: *Deus meus . . . ipse me iussit nasci, ipse dedit mihi salutem per aquam baptismi salutarem, ipse mecum est.*

4

The Crisis and how it was overcome

IN THE FOURTH century there occurred a great crisis in the matter of infant baptism. In 203 in his book *De Paenitentia* Tertullian had been the first sharply to oppose tendencies to postpone repentance and baptism, a postponement based on the desire to enjoy one's life for the meantime and to get the utmost benefit of the forgiveness granted in baptism.[1] Tertullian, be it noted, was addressing himself to pagans who were indeed convinced of the truth of Christianity but hesitated to take the decisive step, a tendency that belongs to the normal experience of every mission. But it will appear that something unparalleled in the normal missionary situation was occurring when we note that this tendency to delay one's conversion to Christianity, if possible till the hour of death in order to die *in albis*, became extremely prevalent in the fourth century; the example of Constantine the Great is well known. Here a superstitious conception of baptism had disastrous results. Since this misunderstanding of baptism increasingly penetrated the churches, even Christian parents began to postpone the baptism of their children; in particular Christian mothers wished to wait till their children had gone through the storms and stresses of youth before they submitted them to the rigorous moral claims of the Church. They feared lest otherwise they might all too easily forfeit the unique gift of baptismal forgiveness and grace. Sins that had been committed before baptism could not endanger salvation since they would be blotted out in baptism. (It was indeed not without peril to delay the baptism of children too long; considering the high rate of child mortality in the ancient world, the risk was great that they might lose their salvation by suddenly dying unbaptized.) The situation is well illustrated by an occurrence which Augustine records in his *Confessions* (397/400) I 11. Between 360 and 370, when he was dangerously ill, his pious mother Monica, who had not had him baptized

[1] See p. 81 above.

at his birth in 354, asked that he might be baptized, but postponed the baptism again when he suddenly recovered, 'because the guilt contracted by sin after baptism would be still greater and more perilous'.[1] In this connection Augustine tells us he has often heard the saying, 'Let him alone, let him do as he pleases, for he is not yet baptized.'[2]

It is now very important to determine at what point of time these tendencies in the churches became prevalent. We can get an answer to this question only by registering the particular cases known to us, in which Christian parents or mothers postponed the baptism of their children. The number of the instances is small since we do not know any biographical details about the mass of ordinary church members.[3] Nevertheless the names that we find are illustrious ones: Basil the Great (born 330/331 in Caesarea in Cappadocia) came of a Christian family, but was not baptized till he was twenty-seven, in the year 358. Ambrose (born in 333/334 or 339/40 in Trier) came from a distinguished Roman family, which boasted of a virgin who had suffered a martyr's death under Diocletian (284–305); his sister took the veil at Epiphany 353; he himself did not seek baptism till 374 after election as bishop. John Chrysostom, born the son of a pious mother in 344/54 in Antioch, did not receive baptism till 368/72. Jerome, born between 340 and 350, the son of Christian parents, in Stridon (Dalmatia), was not baptized until 366 in Rome. Rufinus, born in 345, also a child of a Christian family, in Concordia near Aquileia, did not seek baptism until he was about twenty-five (370). The parents of Paulinus of Nola, who was born about 353 in or near Bordeaux, were Christians also; Paulinus and his brother were not baptized till about 390. Augustine, who was born on 13 November 354 in Thagaste (Numidia), was thirty-two years old when he was baptized on Easter Eve 387. And Gregory of Nazianzus, born in 329/30 near Nazianzus (Cappadocia) who was not baptized till about 360, after a storm on the voyage from Alexandria to Athens had vividly brought before him the danger of a sudden death without baptism, was actually the son of a bishop (who into the bargain let his two other children, his daughter Gorgonia and his second son Caesarius, grow up unbaptized).

---

[1] *Confessiones* I 11: *dilata est itaque mundatio mea, quasi necesse esset, ut adhuc sordidarer, si viverem, quia videlicet post lavacrum illud maior et periculosior in sordibus delictorum reatus foret.*

[2] *Ibid.: sine illum, faciat; nondum enim baptizatus est.*

[3] A contributory factor may be that the postponement of baptism possibly took greater hold in the higher classes of society. 'It appears that in the middle classes and the lowest classes this hesitation [in relation to baptism] was exceptional' is the judgment of V. Schultze, *Altchristliche Städte und Landschaften* III: *Antiocheia*, Gütersloh, 1930, p. 246.

These later very famous theologians, born between 329 and 354, were thus one and all brought up as Christians but not at first baptized. Between East and West, between Cappadocia, Gaul, Syria, Dalmatia, Istria and North Africa there is in this respect, as these eight examples show, no difference. Of great importance, not only for dating the crisis of infant baptism, but also for the history of baptism in general, *is the fact that the earliest case known to us in which Christian parents postponed the baptism of their children, is in the year* 329/30 (Gregory of Nazianzus). The crisis thus begins in the first third of the fourth century and continues through the subsequent decades. As late as 370 the number of such cases in Caesarea in Cappadocia must not have been small, since Basil the Great devoted a whole sermon to persuading people who were not yet baptized, although they had been trained in Christianity from their earliest childhood, to apply for the catechumenate.[1] Gregory of Nyssa (who died soon after 394), the second of the great Cappadocians, addresses a similar audience in his *Oratio adversus eos qui differunt baptisma*.[2] And the third in the group, Gregory of Nazianzus, would not have found it necessary in his famous *Oratio* 40 of 7 January 381, *In sanctum baptisma*,[3] to exhort parents to have their children baptized without delay, if that had then been the general practice. It is significant that he had to deal with the objection that Jesus Christ himself was not baptized till he was thirty years old. The situation is illuminated as by a flash of lightning by a saying which was current at that time: 'Evil threatens us on all sides, let us make haste to baptize our children.'[4]

The epitaphs of the fourth century illustrate this sober evidence by many details, sometimes very touching, which give flesh and blood to our picture of the conditions at that time. Unfortunately their value is sensibly diminished just at this point by the fact that they do not inform us in each particular case whether it is the children of Christian or pagan parents whose memory they preserve.

In the middle of the fourth century a new phenomenon occurs on the tombstone inscriptions—the description of dead persons as neophytes (newly baptized). Until 400 it occurs frequently, and then only in single cases. What interests us here is that the title was also applied to children. From the many instances we choose out those which are dated, and give a complete list of them, so far as they concern children:

[1] *Hom.* 13, *Exhortatoria ad sanctum baptisma* (*MPG* 31, 424-44), Kraft 25–27 (excerpts).
[2] *MPG* 46, 416–32; Kraft 29 f. (excerpt).
[3] Sections 17, 23, 28.
[4] Quoted from Isidore of Pelusium (died about 435), *Epistles* I 125 (*MPG* 78, 265): τοῖς κακοῖς ἐκυκλώθημεν, σπουδαίως τὰ παιδία βαπτίζωμεν.

ILCV I	1477	Rome	348	6 years	8 months		*neofitus*
	1478A	Rome	371	9 years			*neofitus*
	2007	Rome	375	8 years			*neofita*
	1479	Rome	379	5 years			*neofytus*
	1481	Rome	389		8 months		*neofitus*
	1491	Capua	392	1 year	2 months		*neofitus*
				3 years	3 months		*neofitus*
	1494	Bologna	394, 396 or 402	8 years	2 months		*niofitus*
	1501	Milan	402	6 years			*nofitus*

From the use of the title *neofitus* we see that in all these cases baptism was administered shortly before death. Thus all these are cases of baptism *in extremis*, and this explains the considerable variations in the age of the children baptized. In so far as they are children of Christian parents, they are instances of delay of baptism.

We should place in or about the time of Constantine the Great (306–337)[1] the Roman inscription of a boy, Postumius Euthenion, who died at the age of six *gratia sancta consecutus*, and thus was baptized shortly before his death.[2] To the time before 337[3] belongs a Sicilian inscription which tells of a small girl, Julia Florentina, who at the age of eighteen months twenty-two days, at the point of death was given emergency baptism at two o'clock in the morning, but lived four hours longer *ita ut consueta repeteret*—'so that she received the customary rites once again' (*consueta* is an esoteric term used for the Eucharist);[4] the repetition occurred because death was delayed, and as we know, in the fourth and fifth centuries in some places it was reckoned important that the Eucharist should be in the mouth at the moment of the soul's departure.[5] The little girl thus received communion after her emergency baptism and again shortly before her death.[6] A badly defaced inscription on a tomb of a nine-year-old boy belonging to the year 363 mentions his baptism, which leads us to conjecture that it was administered shortly before his death.[7]

[1] Information from A. M. Schneider.
[2] *ILCV* I 1524; Dölger, *Ichthys* I[2] pp. 183–91, Rome.
[3] The inscription gives as the date *Zoilo corr(ectore) p(rovinciae)*. The office of Corrector of the Province of Sicily cannot be traced after Constantine's death in 337. See Th. Mommsen, *Inscriptiones Bruttiorum Lucaniae Campaniae Siciliae Sardiniae Latinae* II (*Corpus Inscriptionum Latinarum* X 2), Berlin, 1883, p. 729, no. 7112; cf. p. 714.
[4] E. Diehl, *Lateinische altchristliche Inschriften* (Kleine Texte 26–28)[2], Bonn, 1913, pp. 6 f. no. 16; *ILCV* I 1549; Dölger, *Ichthys* II 515–35; Kraft 36 f., Catana (Sicily). To Dölger belongs the credit of interpreting the inscription correctly.
[5] Evidence in Dölger, *op. cit.*, 527–35.
[6] For evidence for the communion of young children from the year 251, see above, p. 85 n. 4.
[7] *ILCV* I 1529 note, Rome.

The little girl Fortunia from Capua who died in 371 at the age of about four years, was baptized two days before her death.[1] And lastly we must date to about 400 the sarcophagus inscription of the *infans dulcissima Flavia* who received baptism at Easter at the age of three years and five months, and died five months later (*salutifero die paschae gloriosi fontis gratiam con[sec]uta est superuixitque post baptismum sanctum mensibus quinque*).[2] Of these cases too we may say, in so far as the parents were Christians—which unfortunately we do not know in each particular instance—we have here to do with postponement of baptism.

A more eloquent testimony than that of the direct evidence to the gravity and depth of the crisis is borne by the singular behaviour of the theologians. They are silent. Not that they opposed the practice of infant baptism—of that we have not the slightest evidence. But no one has a clear policy in face of the crisis. In the critical decades after 330 Asterius the Sophist is the only theologian who attests, enjoins and argues for the baptism of the infant children of Christian parents.[3] It is characteristic that so late as 370 Basil the Great and soon afterwards his younger brother, Gregory of Nyssa, while criticizing sharply people who go on postponing baptism,[4] both have adults in mind and do not say a word about infant baptism, although it is reported of Basil that he was ready to baptize children *in extremis*.[5] Was he hindered by the fact that he himself had not been baptized until he grew up?

We dare not, however, infer, from the twofold circumstance that in the fourth century postponement of baptism of children of Christian parents became widely prevalent in the whole Church, and that for the first two thirds of this century (as also for the second half of the third century) there is an almost complete lack of patristic evidence for infant baptism, that the latter had fallen completely out of use in the fourth century. If we put completely out of mind *emergency baptisms* which continued as before to be administered to children,[6] our primary evidence for the survival of infant baptism is in the numerous Church Orders which are

---

[1] *ILCV* I 1525; Kraft 38. The inscription makes the baptism two days after the death. The mason has clearly confused the dates.

[2] E. Diehl, *Lateinische altchristliche Inschriften* p. 4 no. 3; *ILCV* I 1523; F. J. Dölger, 'Die Taufe des Novatian', *Antike und Christentum* II, Münster, 1930, pp. 260–62; Kraft 38, Salona (Dalmatia).

[3] See below, p. 93.

[4] See above, p. 89.

[5] See next note.

[6] For evidence see above, pp. 87 f., 90 f. Theodoret reports a special case, *Hist. Eccl.* (449/50) IV 19.8–10. Basil the Great offers to baptize the dying son of the Emperor Valens (364–78), (παιδίον; Socrates, *Hist. Eccl.* IV 26, *MPG* 67, 533, νήπιος υἱός);

dependent on Hippolytus' Ἀποστολικὴ παράδοσις. We have seen (pp. 73 f.) that much investigation of these still waits to be done. But for all that we can already say today that, after its appearance about the year 215, Hippolytus' *Apostolic Tradition* entered upon a veritable march of triumph and conquered great parts of the Church of that day. We know this, because with greater or lesser modifications it became a part or a source of many books on canon law:[1] a Latin book somewhere about the end of the fourth century; the eighth book of the Greek *Apostolic Constitutions* (370/380, Syria) and a text parallel thereto named *Epitome* or *Canones per Hippolytum*; the Sahidic so-called *Canones Ecclesiastici*;[2] the *Testamentum Domini*, originally Greek, probably fifth-century from Syria;[3] the *Canones Hippolyti*, originally Greek, about AD 500.[4] Here one must note that the various Church Orders all codify an older usage; the date of their composition is thus a *terminus ante quem*. If then the Church Orders here named reproduce without exception[5] the regulation discussed above on pp. 74 f., about the administration of infant baptism,[6] this shows that the custom of baptizing infants (*infantes, infantes parvi, νήπια*) continued *unbroken*.

But the Church Orders are by no means our only evidence. For the West we have also the decisions of the Synod of Elvira in southern Spain (306/12),[7] and above all tombstone inscriptions, proving that in the fourth century as before, infant baptism was administered to the

but Valens has the baptism administered by Arians who were present. The parallels, Gregory of Nazianzus, *Oratio* 43 *in laudem Basilii Magni*, 54 (*MPG* 36, 564 f.); Rufinus, *Hist. Eccl.* II 9 (*MPL* 21, 519 f.); Socrates, *loc. cit.*; Sozomen, *Hist. Eccl.* VI 16 (*MPG* 67, 1332 f.), say only that Basil offered to pray for the boy.

[1] Cf. the survey on pp. 13 f.

[2] They are also preserved in several Arabic translations, in Ethiopic and Bohairic translations, and the latter re-translated into Arabic.

[3] The book is only preserved in Syriac, Arabic (after a Coptic original) and in Ethiopic, with some sections also in Latin.

[4] They are only preserved in Arabic and Ethiopic, with probably a Coptic intermediary.

[5] Unfortunately the corresponding passage in the Latin book has not been preserved. In the *Apostolic Constitutions* the whole passage of the Church Order dealing with baptism is missing, but in VI 15.7 comes the instruction, βαπτίζετε δὲ ὑμῶν καὶ τὰ νήπια.

[6] Texts in Kraft 16 f.; survey see above pp. 13 f.

[7] Canon 1 (*De his qui post baptismum idolis immolaverunt*): Communion is refused to those who after baptism *adulta aetate* offered sacrifice to idols, even on their deathbeds. From the limitation of the rule to adults we conclude that baptized young children, who were not yet responsible, are granted freedom from penalty. Canon 22 (*De catholicis in haeresim transeuntibus, si revertantur*): appended to the resolution that members of the Church who had fallen into heresy (*si quis de catholica ecclesia ad haeresim transitum fecerit rursusque ad ecclesiam recurrerit*) should not be admitted again to communion until they had done penance for ten years, it is written: *si vero infantes fuerint transducti, quod non suo vitio peccaverint incunctanter recipi debent*. From the expression *transducti* we may conclude that the *infantes* had been made members of the Church by baptism, before they were led into heresy.

children of Christian parents, since we find at this period numerous inscriptions concerning infants who obviously were baptized at birth.[1] For the East until recently the Church Orders were our only evidence, but at last a new discovery has closed this gap and shown us how careful one must be with the *argumentum e silentio*. M. Richard has succeeded in proving that thirty-one homilies which some manuscripts intersperse in Chrysostom's *Commentary on Psalms* 4–12, and of which seven are quoted in a Palestinian catena and ascribed to 'Asterius the Arian', belong in great part to Asterius 'the Arian' or 'the Sophist' (died after 341).[2] *Homily* 12.3 f. on Ps. 6, 21.10 on Ps. 11, and 27.2 f. on Ps. 14[3] mention infant baptism.[4] In these three homilies, written before the middle of the fourth century, it is presupposed as customary in the church of the author.[5] The duty of having their children baptized is impressed on parents.[6] Asterius came from Cappadocia, studied under Lucian of Antioch and is last met with at a synod in Antioch in 341. So we discover to our astonishment that at the same time and in the same country for which we have reliable evidence for the postponement of baptism (see p. 88 on John Chrysostom and the Cappadocians, Basil and Gregory Nazianzus) we find the baptism of newborn infants as the normal practice.

An important proof that, even during the crisis of the fourth century, infant baptism continued to be administered without interruption is given us finally by the fact that the *heretics* administered it at this time. For the East the Arian Asterius bears witness that the Arians baptized βρέφη just as did the 'heterodox', and the Donatist Cresconius informs us that the Jewish-Christian Symmachians both circumcised and baptized

---

[1] The following examples from *ILCV* II: 3 months old (3263, Thysdrus, Africa: *in pace Xρ*); 7 months (2945 B, Rome, dated 389: *in pace*); 7 months (3254, Rome: *in pace Xρ*); 7 months (3080 A, Salona: *in [pace]*); 10 months (3054, Rome; <two doves> . . . *inno Xρ cens*); 11 months (2969 A, Rome, 379: *A Xρ Ω* . . . <dove with garland> . . . *in pace*); 11 months (2967, Rome, 361: *in pace*); three from *ILCV* I: 1 year 2 months (1404 A, Furni, Africa: *fidelis in pace*); 2 years 6 months (1344, near Capua, 346, *fidelis Deo*); 4 years 2 days (1334, Clusium, 343, 354, 365 or 376: *cristaeanus fidelis*); 4 years 8 months (*ILCV* II 3354, Rome, *accersitus ab angelis*). We must note again that (as in the instances given on pp. 55 f., 75–80, 85 f. as evidence for the third century) the information about age gives the age at death, not at baptism. That in these cases baptism was administered at birth, is A. M. Schneider's inference from the absence of the attribute *neofitus*.

[2] See list of sources.

[3] These baptismal passages were already noticed by J.-C. Didier, 'Le pédobaptisme au IVe siècle. Documents nouveaux', *MelScR* 6, 1949, pp. 245 f.

[4] M. Richard ascribes *Hom.* 12 and 21 without doubt to Asterius. *Hom.* 27 he divides into two parts (1–8, 9–24), of which the first, with the evidence for baptism, also probably comes from Asterius (p. viii).

[5] J.-C. Didier, *op. cit.*, p. 241.

[6] *Hom.* 12.4.

their children;[1] for the West we learn from Canon 48 of the Third
Synod of Carthage (397) that among the Donatists who broke away from
the Church in 312 the *infantes* were likewise baptized. In both cases the
texts give us to know that the usage in itself was no peculiarity of the
heretics; they did not introduce it as a novelty after their breakaway from
the Great Church, but took it over from the latter. Further, both Augustine[2] and Pelagius[3] say that they had never heard of a schismatic or heretic
who had renounced the baptism of *infantes* or *parvuli*.

After about 365 the literary sources suddenly begin to flow freely.[4]
The baptism of newborn infants is cited[5] as a well-established custom,
enjoined[6] and theologically justified,[7] as if nothing had happened.

From all the wealth of evidence before us let us take one example each
from North Africa, Italy, Palestine, Byzantium and Egypt. In North
Africa, about 365, Optatus of Milevis (Numidia) presupposes infant
baptism as an accepted usage, when, describing Christ as the garment
which the Christian puts on in baptism, he says 'It shows no crease when
infants put it on, it is not too scanty for young men, it fits women without
alteration.'[8] Ambrose of Milan justifies baptism by appealing to the Old
Testament ordinance of infant circumcision[9] and cites John 3.5 to justify

---

[1] See above, p. 48.

[2] *De peccatorum meritis et remissione et de baptismo parvulorum ad Marcellinum* III
6.12 (412) (*MPL* 44, 192 f.; *CSEL* 60, p. 139).

[3] In Augustine, *De gratia Christi et de peccato originali* II 18.20 (418) (*MPL* 44,
395; *CSEL* 42, pp. 180 f.).

[4] Cf. the survey of sources, pp. 15–18.

[5] Zeno of Verona, *Tractatus* I 13 (362/72); Optatus of Milevis (Numidia), *Contra
Parmenianum Donatistam* V 10 (about 365); Didymus the Blind, *De Trinitate* II 14
(381/92); Pope Siricius, ep. I (dated 10.2.385); Ambrose, *Exposition of Luke* I 36–38
(385/89); Sixth Synod of Carthage (September 401), Canon 7; Synod of Rome (402),
Canon 5; Innocent I, *epp.* 3, 25 and 30 (dated 415–17); Mark the Deacon, *Life of
Porphyry* 31–47 (after 420); Cyril of Alexandria, *Comm. on John* VII (cited below,
p. 95 n. 4). (For fuller references see the list of sources, pp. 11 f.) We must of course
pay no attention to those references in which *infans* has the metaphorical significance
'newly baptized person', as for example *Itinerarium Burdigalense* (333) 594 (*Itinera
Hierosolymitana saeculi IIII–VIII, CSEL* 39, p. 23): [in the Church of the Holy
Sepulchre in Jerusalem] *balneum a tergo, ubi infantes lauantur;* Paulinus of Nola, *ep.*
32 (*CSEL* 29, p. 280) (392): *inde parens sacro ducit de fonte sacerdos infantes niveos
corpore corde habitu;* Egeria, *Peregrinatio ad loca sancta* (about 417), 38.1 (*Itinera
Hierosolymitana* p. 90): *infantes, cum baptidiati fuerint et vestiti, quemadmodum exierint
de fonte . . . ;* 39.3 (p. 91): *episcopus cum omni clero et omnibus infantibus, id est qui
baptidiati fuerint . . .*

[6] In *Const. Apost.* VI 15.7, cited on p. 92 n. 5; also by Siricius, Sixth Synod of
Carthage and Innocent I, see previous note.

[7] By Ambrose, *De Abraham* II 11.81.84 (387); Chrysostom, *Hom. in Gen.* 40.4 (388);
Hom. ad neophytos, quoted in Augustine, *Contra Iulianum Pelagianum* I 6.21 f.; and
above all Augustine himself.   [8] *Contra Parmenianum* V 10.

[9] *De Abraham* II 11.81. Before him Zeno of Verona said in an Easter sermon: *haec*
[baptism as *secunda circumcisio*] *a cunis* (from the cradle) *ipsis infantiae usque ad supremos
exitus cuiusvis aetatis utrique generi salutare munus impertit* (*Tractatus* I 13).

his doubt whether small children (*infantes*) dying without baptism have a share in the Kingdom of Heaven.[1] In a letter written about 400 from Bethlehem to Laeta Jerome asserts that it is a grievous sin in Christian parents not to bring their *infantes* for baptism.[2] In 388 Chrysostom in Constantinople in the *Homily to Neophytes* lauds the *baptismatis largitates* and draws therefrom the conclusion 'Therefore we baptize little children (τὰ παιδία) also, although they have no sin.'[3] And in 428 Cyril of Alexandria, commenting on John 11.26, remarks that the words 'Believest thou this?' demand a confession of faith like the Amen which the father speaks 'when a newborn child is brought forward to receive the anointing of initiation, or rather of consummation through holy baptism.'[4] Thus he bears witness, as did his fellow-countryman Didymus the Blind some forty years earlier (he was head of the Catechetical School at Alexandria from *c.* 350 to 398), that in Egypt also infant baptism was the rule at that time.[5] To this time also belongs our first certain evidence of the baptism of an infant of Caesar's family—Theodosius II (408–450), born in October 401, was baptized in Byzantium not long after his birth.[6]

The dating of the crisis, which we have established, is instructive for the understanding of it. We have seen that the first demonstrable instance of Christian parents postponing the baptism of their children was in the year 329/30 (see p. 89), and that the ecclesiastical reaction against the postponement of baptism began about 365. The acute crisis, therefore, lies in the decades following the recognition of Christianity as the religion of the state, i.e. in that period during which countless numbers of pagans were flocking into the Church. It is no surprise to find that the superstitious conception of baptism which many of these pagans brought with them also had an influence upon Christian circles.

[1] *De Abraham* II 11.84: *nisi quis renatus fuerit ex aqua et spiritu sancto, non potest introire in regnum dei* (John 3.5): *utique nullum excipit, non infantem, non aliqua praeventum necessitate.*

[2] *Ep.* 107.6.—From Gaza the *Life of Porphyry*, composed after Porphyry's death (26.2.420) by his secretary, Mark the Deacon, and rhetorically written up in the sixth century, informs, us of an infant baptism on the conversion of a family about 399. A heathen woman, who was in danger of a miscarriage, was happily delivered by the aid of Porphyry. The next day with her parents, her husband and all her kinsfolk she entered the catechumenate. 'And after a short time he (Porphyry) baptized them together with the woman, after he had instructed them, and also the child (κατηχήσας αὐτοὺς ἐβάπτισεν σὺν τῇ γυναικὶ καὶ τὸ βρέφος). And they called the child Porphyry.'

[3] Cited in Augustine, *Contra Iulianum Pelagianum* (422) I 6.22: διὰ τοῦτο καὶ τὰ παιδία βαπτίζομεν, καίτοι ἁμαρτήματα οὐκ ἔχοντα.

[4] *Comm. on John* VII on 11.26 (*MPG* 74, 49): ὅτε γὰρ ἀρτιγενὲς προσάγεται βρέφος τῆς κατηχήσεως τὸ χρῖσμα λαβεῖν, ἤτοι τὸ τῆς τελειώσεως ἐπὶ τῷ ἁγίῳ βαπτίσματι. . . .

[5] *De Trinitate* II 14: (Baptism purifies from all previous sins.) πρὸς ἐπὶ τούτοις, πάντας ἐκ χάριτος ἀδελφοὺς πρωτοτόκους καὶ ἀρτιτόκους, καὶ αὐτοὺς τοὺς ἐξ ἡλικας καὶ ἀφήλικας ἀναδείκνυσι.

[6] Mark the Deacon, *Life of Porphyry* 44–47.

A certain influence of the crisis is visible, but only in Gregory of Nazianzus' *Oratio* 40 *in sanctum baptisma*[1] already mentioned, delivered on 7 January 381 in Constantinople. He is indeed far from having serious doubts (sec. 17: νήπιον ἔστι σοι; . . . ἐκ βρέφους ἁγιασθήτω); at all events, where life is in danger we should not hesitate.[2] However, he advises that children should normally be baptized at about the age of three 'when they can take in something of the mystery, and answer [the baptismal questions], and even if they do not yet understand fully, can nevertheless retain some impression'.[3] This justification is 'typically Greek'.[4] It is no coincidence that when we have evidence of children being dedicated in the mystery religions,[5] we have repeated cases of children younger than seven years old (three times we hear of children who died at the age of seven who had been dedicated),[6] but we hear nothing of infants. It seems to me that it was a source of error when these parallels from the history of Hellenistic religion were introduced in days past into the debate on the problem of infant baptism, in order to throw light upon, and increase our understanding of apostolic times. They were influential not in the first century after Christ—even though at an early period other Hellenistic influences were at work in the practice of baptism—but rather in the fourth.[7]

We have, however, no grounds for believing that the advice which Gregory of Nazianzus gave in 381, to postpone the baptism of children to the age of three years, had any influence on church practice beyond a limited area or for any length of time. When the little Flavia, as we saw on p. 91, received baptism about 400 in Salona (Dalmatia) at the age of three years and five months, the agreement between her age and Gregory's recommendations was probably pure coincidence.

[1] See above, pp. 89 f.   [2] Sec. 28.

[3] *Ibid.*: περὶ δὲ τῶν ἄλλων [children who have no need of emergency baptism], δίδωμι γνώμην, τὴν τριετίαν ἀναμείναντας, ἢ μικρὸν ἐντὸς τούτου, ἢ ὑπὲρ τοῦτο (ἡνίκα καὶ ἀκοῦσαί τι μυστικόν, καὶ ἀποκρίνεσθαι δυνατόν, εἰ καὶ μὴ συνιέντα τελέως, ἀλλ᾽ οὖν τυπούμενα), οὕτως ἁγιάζειν καὶ ψυχὰς καὶ σώματα τῷ μεγάλῳ μυστηρίῳ τῆς τελειώσεως.

[4] H. Windisch, 'Zum Problem der Kindertaufe im Urchristentum', *ZNW* 28, 1929, p. 139.

[5] A. Oepke, 'Zur Frage nach dem Ursprung der Kindertaufe', *L. Ihmels-Festschrift*, pp. 92–94, especially the important collection of material, p. 92 n. 6; J. Leipoldt, *Die Urchristliche Taufe*, Leipzig, 1928, pp. 74–78; A. Oepke, ΑΜΦΙΘΑΛΕΙΣ im griechischen und hellenistischen Kult', *Archiv für Religionswissenschaft* 31, 1934, pp. 42–56, esp. p. 55 n. 4; 'Die Kindertaufe—eine Wunde unserer Kirche?', *Evangelisch-Lutherische Kirchenzeitung* 1947, p. 30.

[6] A. Oepke, 'Urchristentum und Kindertaufe', *ZNW* 29, 1930, p. 91; L. Ihmels-*Festschrift*, p. 92 n. 6.

[7] F. J. Dölger also, 'Die Taufe des Novatian', *Antike und Christentum* II, Münster, 1930, pp. 258–67, assumes that Gregory of Nazianzus (as also Basil) was consciously or unconsciously influenced by older views (p. 263). In addition the views of his father on baptism (see above, p. 88) may have been of influence on him.

During the Pelagian conflicts the crisis was finally overcome, thanks to the dominating personality of Augustine. At this period there are frequent synodal decrees which mention infant baptism. The sixteenth Synod of Carthage (418) hurls its anathema against anyone who 'says that newly-born infants should not be baptized' (*parvulos recentes ab uteris matrum baptizandos negat*).[1] How heated in these years in North Africa feeling was among simple people can be seen from a drastic remark of Augustine, who cries out in 422 to the Pelagians that they would have reason to fear that men would spit in their faces and women would throw their sandals at their heads if they dared to say of *infantes*, 'Let them not be baptized' (*non baptizentur*).[2]

[1] Canon 2 (Hardouin I 927, 1217 f.; Kraft, p. 18). According to tradition the canon is also cited as the second canon of the Second Synod of Milevis (416) (Hardouin I 1217; so also Kraft, *ibid.*), but wrongly (cf. C. J. von Hefele, *Conciliengeschichte* II². Freiburg im Breisgau, 1875, p. 113 n. 3).
[2] *Contra Iulianum Pelagianum* III 5.11 (*MPL* 44, 708).

5

Conclusion

IN THIS WORK an attempt has been made to place before the reader as completely as possible the material on our theme 'Infant Baptism in the First Four Centuries', and the author hopes that nothing essential has escaped him. A thorough examination of all the sources makes it quite clear that in this whole period of four centuries there were to be found only two theologians who advocated a postponement of baptism, both of them, moreover, with reservations. Tertullian's advice in *De Baptismo* to delay baptism related to the children of pagan parents, and in addition made an exception of emergency baptism, and Gregory of Nazianzus recommended merely the postponement of baptism to the age of about three years. Even more striking is another circumstance: while many theological grounds are adduced in favour of infant baptism—with reference to the blessing of the children in Matt. 19.13-15, to John 3.5, to the blessings of salvation bestowed in baptism, to the analogy of the ordinance of circumcision, and above all with reference to original sin (Origen, Cyprian and Tertullian in *De Anima*)—neither of the two above-mentioned advocates of postponement of baptism offers any theological justification. Rather does Tertullian appeal to the innocence of children (*innocens aetas*), which he claims makes haste unnecessary, and to the undue responsibility laid upon the shoulders of godparents standing sponsor for the Christian upbringing of the children of pagans, while Gregory of Nazianzus adduces in self-justification only the wish that the children should at least be able 'to take in something of the mystery', themselves to answer and to receive an impression. Certainly the large numbers of Christian parents in the fourth century who postponed the baptism of their children till they had got through the storms and stresses of youth were not moved by serious theological considerations, but were influenced by a magical misunderstanding of baptism.

With these concluding remarks problems are indicated which lie beyond the scope of our investigation, because they can only be treated significantly if we do not limit ourselves to infant baptism, but take into consideration the development of the whole doctrine of baptism in the first four centuries.

ABBREVIATIONS

ANCL	Ante-Nicene Christian Library, Edinburgh.
Billerbeck	H. L. Strack and P. Billerbeck, *Kommentar zum Neuen Testament aus Talmud und Midrasch* I–V, Munich, 1922–28, 1956.
BZNW	Beihefte zur *Zeitschrift für die Neutestamentliche Wissenschaft*, Berlin.
CIG	*Corpus Inscriptionum Graecarum* IV 1–2, ed. A. Boeckh, J. Franz, E. Curtius and A. Kirchhoff, Berlin, 1877.
CII	*Corpus Inscriptionum Iudaicarum* I–II (Sussidi allo studio delle antichità cristiane 1.3), ed. J.-B. Frey, Rome and Paris, 1936, 1952.
CSEL	*Corpus Scriptorum Ecclesiasticorum Latinorum*, Vienna, Prague and Leipzig.
F. J. Dölger,	*Ichthys Das Fisch-Symbol in frühchristlicher Zeit* (*Ichthys* I), Münster, 1910,² 1928.
	Der Heilige Fisch in den antiken Religionen und im Christentum : Text (*Ichthys* II), Münster, 1922.
	The same : Plates (*Ichthys* III), Münster, 1922.
	Die Fisch-Denkmäler in der frühchristlichen Plastik, Malerei und Kleinkunst (*Ichthys* V), Münster, 1943.
ET	English translation.
ExpT	*Expository Times*, Edinburgh.
GCS	*Die Griechischen Christlichen Schriftsteller der ersten Jahrhunderte*, Leipzig and Berlin.
Hardouin	J. Hardouin, *Acta conciliorum et epistolae decretales, ac constitutiones summorum pontificum* I, Paris, 1715.
ILCV	*Inscriptiones Latinae Christianae Veteres* I–III, ed. E. Diehl, Berlin, 1925–31.
JBL	*Journal of Biblical Literature*, Philadelphia.
JQR	*Jewish Quarterly Review*, London.
JTS	*Journal of Theological Studies*, Oxford.
Kraft	H. Kraft, *Texte zur Geschichte der Taufe, besonders der Kindertaufe in der alten Kirche* (Kleine Texte 174), Berlin, 1953.
MelScR	*Mélanges de Science Religieuse*, Lille.
MPG	Migne, *Patrologia Graeca*, Paris.
MPL	Migne, *Patrologia Latina*, Paris.
N.F.	Neue Folge.
NPNF	Nicene and Post-Nicene Fathers, Oxford and New York.
NTS	*New Testament Studies*, Oxford.

RAC	*Reallexicon für Antike und Christentum*, Stuttgart, 1950 ff.
RB	*Revue Biblique*, Paris.
RHPR	*Revue d'Histoire et de Philosophie Religieuses*, Paris.
SBT	Studies in Biblical Theology, London.
SC	Sources Chrétiennes, Paris.
ST	*Studia Theologica*, Lund.
TLZ	*Theologische Literaturzeitung*, Berlin.
TS	Texts and Studies, Cambridge.
TU	Texte und Untersuchungen, Leipzig and Berlin.
TWNT	*Theologisches Wörterbuch zum Neuen Testament*, Stuttgart, 1933 ff.
TZ	*Theologische Zeitschrift*, Basle.
WZU Leipzig	*Wissenschaftliche Zeitschrift der Karl-Marx Universität Leipzig*, Gesellschafts- und sprachwissenschaftliche Reihe, Leipzig.
ZNW	*Zeitschrift für die Neutestamentliche Wissenschaft*, Berlin.
ZTK	*Zeitschrift für Theologie und Kirche*, Tübingen.

ı6635
BIBLIOGRAPHY

J. LIGHTFOOT, *Horae Hebraicae et Talmudicae*, 1658 ff., on Matt. 3.6.

W. WALL, *The History of Infant-Baptism*, London, 1674 (cited from the two-volume ed., London, 1705. Most recent ed. in The Ancient and Modern Library of Theological Literature, 2 vols., London, 1889).

J. W. H. HÖFLING, *Das Sakrament der Taufe nebst den anderen damit zusammenhängenden Akten der Initiation* I, Erlangen, 1846, pp. 98–126.

F. BOISSIÈRE, *Le paedobaptisme ou baptême des enfants est-il évangélique?*, Strassburg, 1848.

R. CLÉMENT, *Etude biblique sur le baptême ou le pédobaptisme et l'Eglise*, Lausanne, 1857.

J. CORBLET, *Histoire dogmatique, liturgique et archéologique du sacrement du baptême*, 2 vols., Geneva, 1881–2.

E. MÉNÉGOZ, 'Le baptême des enfants d'après les principes de la théologie paulinienne', *Revue Chrétienne* (Paris) 31, 1884, pp. 234–48.

F. J. DÖLGER, *Der Exorcismus im altchristlichen Taufritual* (Studien zur Geschichte und Kultur des Altertums 3.1–2), Paderborn, 1909, pp. 39–43.

H. G. WOOD, 'Baptism (Later Christian)', *Encyclopaedia of Religion and Ethics* II, Edinburgh, 1909, pp. 390–406; here pp. 392–95.

G. BAREILLE, 'Baptême II: Baptême d'après les pères grecs et latins', *Dictionnaire de Théologie Catholique* II, Paris, 1910, cols. 178–219; here cols. 192–96.

F. J. DÖLGER, *Ichthys* I, Münster, 1910,[2] 1928, pp. 183–91 (ΙΧΘΥC ΝΗΠΙΩΝ or ΝΕΟΚΤΙCΤΩΝ, ΝΕΟΦΩΤΙCΤΩΝ?); pp. 192–203 (funerary inscriptions with ΙΧΘΥC and indirect reference to infant baptism). ΙΧΘΥC II, Münster, 1922, pp. 515–35 (*Mysterium fidei*. On the history of the Last Sacrament): ΙΧΘΥC V, Münster, 1932–43, pp. 728–30 (the fish in inscriptions about neophytes).

Idem, 'Die Taufe Konstantins und ihre Probleme', in *Konstantin der Grosse und seine Zeit*, ed. Dölger (Römische Quartalschrift, Supplementary vol. 19), Freiburg im Breisgau, 1913, pp. 377–447, here pp. 429–37 (the late baptism of Constantine judged as a custom of the period).

TH. SCHERMANN, *Die allgemeine Kirchenordnung, frühchristliche Liturgien und kirchliche Überlieferung* II: *Frühchristliche Liturgien* (Studien zur Geschichte und Kultur des Altertums, 3, suppl. vol. 2), Paderborn, 1915, pp. 268–71.

R. SEEBERG, *Lehrbuch der Dogmengeschichte* I[3], Leipzig and Erlangen, 1922, pp. 451 f.

G. POLSTER, 'Der kleine Talmudtraktat über die Proselyten', *Angelos* (Leipzig) 2, 1926, pp. 1–38.

A. OEPKE, 'Zur Frage nach dem Ursprung der Kindertaufe', in *Das Erbe Martin Luthers und die gegenwärtige theologische Forschung* (Festschrift for L. Ihmels), Leipzig, 1928, pp. 84–100.

J. LEIPOLDT, *Die urchristliche Taufe im Lichte der Religionsgeschichte*, Leipzig, 1928, pp. 23 f., 73–78.

H. WINDISCH, 'Zum Problem der Kindertaufe im Urchristentum', *ZNW* 28, 1929, pp. 118–42.

F. J. DÖLGER, 'Die Taufe des Novatian', in *Antike und Christentum* II, Munster, 1930, pp. 258–67.

T. S. HALL, *Is Infant Baptism Scriptural?* [3], London, 1930.

A. OEPKE, 'Urchristentum und Kindertaufe', *ZNW* 29, 1930, pp. 81–111.

Idem, '*βάπτω* etc.', *TWNT* I, 1933, pp. 527–44, here p. 541.

B. SUNDKLER, *Huru gammalt är Barndopets Sakrament?*, Uppsala, 1933.

O. CULLMANN, 'Les traces d'une vieille formule baptismale dans le Nouveau Testament', *RHPR* 17, 1937, pp. 424–34.

J. JEREMIAS, *Hat die älteste Christenheit die Kindertaufe geübt?*, Göttingen, 1938; *Hat die Urkirche die Kindertaufe geübt?* [2], Göttingen, 1949.

J. G. DAVIES, *Infant Baptism, History and Modern Practice*, London, 1939.

D. A. FRÖVIG, 'Har den eldste kristenhet hatt barnedåp?', *Tidsskrift for Teologi og Kirche* (Oslo) 11, 1940, pp. 124–31.

H. H. ROWLEY, 'Jewish Proselyte Baptism and the Baptism of John', *Hebrew Union College Annual* (Cincinnati, Ohio) 15, 1940, pp. 313–34.

J. JEREMIAS, 'Mc 10.13–16 Parr. und die Übung der Kindertaufe in der Urkirche', *ZNW* 40, 1941, pp. 243–45.

H. G. MARSH, *The Origin and Significance of the New Testament Baptism*, Manchester, 1941, pp. 174–80.

E. STAUFFER, *New Testament Theology*, ET London, 1955 (originally 1941), pp. 161 f., 298 f.

E. MOLLAND, 'Barnedåpens oprinnelse og alder', *Norsk Teologisk Tidsskrift* (Oslo) 43, 1942, pp. 1–23.

K. BARTH, *The Teaching of the Church regarding Baptism*, ET London, 1948 (originally 1943).

G. MIEGGE, *Il battesimo dei fanciulli nella storia, nella teoria, nella prassi*, Torre Pellice, n.d. (about 1943).

O. CULLMANN, *Early Christian Worship* (Studies in Biblical Theology 10), ET London, 1953 (originally 1944).

H. GROSSMANN, *Ein Ja zur Kindertaufe* (Kirchliche Zeitfragen 13), Zurich, 1944.

F.-J. LEENHARDT, *Le baptême chrétien. Son origine, sa signification* (Cahiers théologiques de l'Actualité protestante 4), Neuchâtel and Paris, 1946, pp. 66–73.

G. C. BERKOUWER, *Karl Barth en de kinderdoop*, Kampen, 1947.

G. C. VAN NIFTRIK, 'De kinderdoop en Karl Barth', *Nederlands Theologisch Tijdschrift* (Wageningen), 2, 1947/48, pp. 18–43.

A. OEPKE, 'Die Kindertaufe—eine Wunde unserer Kirche?', *Evangelisch-lutherische Kirchenzeitung* (Munich) 1, 1947, pp. 29–35.

TH. PREISS, 'Le baptême des enfants et le Nouveau Testament', *Verbum Caro* (Neuchâtel) 1, 1947, pp. 113–22; reprinted in *La Vie en Christ*,

Neuchâtel and Paris, 1951, pp. 132–43—'Die Kindertaufe und das Neue Testament', *TLZ* 73, 1948, cols. 651–60.

H. SCHLIER, 'Zur kirchlichen Lehre von der Taufe', *TLZ* 72, 1947, cols. 321–36.

O. CULLMANN, *Baptism in the New Testament* (Studies in Biblical Theology 1), ET London, 1950 (originally 1948).

W. F. FLEMINGTON, *The New Testament Doctrine of Baptism*, London, 1948, pp. 130–47.

PH.-H. MENOUD, 'Le baptême des enfants dans l'Eglise ancienne', *Verbum Caro* (Neuchâtel), 2, 1948, pp. 15–26.

A. BENOIT, 'Le problème du pédobaptisme', *RHPR* 28–29, 1948–49, pp. 132–41 (bibliography).

P. ALTHAUS, 'Was ist die Taufe? Zur Antwort an Karl Barth', *TLZ* 74, 1949, cols. 705–14.

J.-J. VON ALLMEN, 'Luc (9.37–43a) et le baptême des enfants', *Foi et Vie* (Paris), 47, 1949, pp. 59–75.

J.-C. DIDIER, 'Le pédobaptisme au IVe siècle. Documents nouveaux', *MelScR* 6, 1949, pp. 233–46.

J. JEREMIAS, 'Proselytentaufe und Neues Testament', *TZ* 5, 1949, pp. 418–28.

F.-J. LEENHARDT, 'Le baptême des enfants et le Nouveau Testament', *Foi et Vie* 47, 1949, pp. 76–91.

J. LEIPOLDT, 'Zur Kindertaufe', *TLZ* 74, 1949, cols. 139 f.

W. MICHAELIS, 'Die jüdische Proselytentaufe und die Tauflehre des Neuen Testaments', *Kirchenblatt für die Reformierte Schweiz* (Basel) 105, 1949, pp. 17–20, 34–38.

E. STAUFFER, 'Zur Kindertaufe in der Urkirche', *Deutsches Pfarrerblatt* (Essen) 49, 1949, pp. 152–54.

J.-J. VON ALLMEN, 'L'Eglise primitive et le baptême des enfants', *Verbum Caro* 4, 1950, pp. 43–47.

P. BRUNNER, *Aus der Kraft des Werkes Christi. Zur Lehre von der heiligen Taufe und vom heiligen Abendmahl* (Kirchlich-theologische Hefte 9), Munich, 1950, pp. 39–41.

J. HÉRING, 'Un texte oublié: Matthieu 18.10. A propos des controverses récentes sur le pédobaptisme', in *Aux sources de la tradition chrétienne* (Mélanges offerts à M. M. Goguel), Neuchâtel and Paris, 1950, pp. 95–102.

W. G. KÜMMEL, 'Das Urchristentum. Nachträge zu Teil I–III', *Theologische Rundschau* (Tübingen) 18, 1950, pp. 1–53, here pp. 32–47.

F.-J. LEENHARDT, *Pédobaptisme catholique et pédobaptisme réformé* (Études Théologiques et Religieuses [Montpellier] 25), 1950.

F. LOVSKY, 'Notes d'histoire pour contribuer à l'étude du problème baptismal', *Foi et Vie* 48, 1950, pp. 109–38.

M. BARTH, *Die Taufe—ein Sakrament?* Zurich, 1951, pp. 163 f.

J.-C. DIDIER, 'Un cas typique de développement du dogme. A propos du baptême des enfants', *MelScR* 9, 1952, pp. 191–214 (bibliography).

J. SCHNEIDER, *Die Taufe im Neuen Testament*, Stuttgart, 1952 (reviewed by A. Oepke, *TLZ* 79, 1954, cols. 101–4).

H. KRAFT, *Texte zur Geschichte der Taufe, besonders der Kindertaufe in der Alten Kirche* (Kleine Texte 174), Berlin, 1953.

P. CH. MARCEL, *The Biblical Doctrine of Infant Baptism*, ET London, 1953 (originally 1950).

J. LEIPOLDT, 'Die altchristliche Taufe religionsgeschichtlich betrachtet', *WZU Leipzig* 3, 1953/54, pp. 63–74.

A. OEPKE, 'παῖς etc.', *TWNT* V, 1954, pp. 636–53, here pp. 646 f., 649 f.

J. DUPLACY, 'Le salut par la foi et le baptême d'après le Nouveau Testament', *Lumière et Vie* (Saint-Alban-Leysse, Savoie) 27, July 1956, pp. 291–340.

W. METZGER, 'Wird in I Kor. 7.14c ein Tauf versicht sichtbar?', *Deutsches Pfarrerblatt* 59, 1959, pp. 269–71.

INDEX OF BIBLICAL REFERENCES

INDEX OF SOURCES

INDEX OF MODERN AUTHORS

INDEX OF SUBJECTS